# PowerShell Source Code: Winmgmts ExecNotificationQuery

Using ___InstanceModificationEvent

By Richard Thomas Edwards

# CONTENTS

# Introduction

## Why another book on PowerShell?

I really put some thought into that question. For about 2 minutes and then started to write it. Fact is, I don't need a reason for writing this book. Because it really isn't a book, it is 100 pages of source code you simply can't afford to not to use.

I'm not saying you have to buy my book, I'm saying that the reason why I am writing this book is because, like you, I was once in your shoes looking for that one perfect example no how to get through a sticky point in my coding experience that not only worked for me, it worked for my customers who were developers and being supported by Microsoft Technical Support.

Back then, that single chapter, that one little piece of information, cost me $50. Today, you're looking at being able to get the same for a measly $3.99 for the E-book and around $14.95 for the Paperback.

The problem that I have is, in order to fill 100 pages, I have to use the same routines across every other book I am writing. Otherwise, you don't get a nice size book of coding examples and I don't get paid enough money to cover my time and effort producing these books.

So, please excuse the canned content that I've added as example code using GWMI. It is needed to give you that kernel of code you will need to make the code work for you.

# What WMI namespaces and classes are on your machine?

Someone once said, "It is what you don't know that can kill you," Well, they might not have said it exactly that way, but you get the idea.

How can you use something that exists on your machine, but you don't know it?

Back in 2002, I created something called the WMI Explorer. Microsoft came out with their version in May of 2003. Neither one of us cared, It pretty much fell flat on its face.

The biggest difference between the two is my class groupings was based on the way the classes were presented. In-other-words, I there was no underscore, the category was the classname. If there was an underscore at the beginning of the classname, it was a superclass. It there was an underscore in the middle of the classname, the letters before the underscore became its category.

I thought it was a pretty good idea at the time.

Apparently, no one else did. Fact is, the concept was never used by anyone else and WMI Explorer that other people began to "create" used the Microsoft template and never did consider a more granular approach.

I also think the other reason why the WMI Explorer didn't become popular was because of the lack of documentation beyond the most common root: root\cimv2. And back in 2003 time, there were less than a few hundred of them.

But today is a completely different ballpark. Today there are literally hundreds of classes under root\cimv2 alone.

Would you like your own personal copy?

The following scripts that I've been using since 2002, will make that happen for you. Just create a folder on your desktop, then copy and paste the three scripts into that directory and start with namespaces.vbs and end with classes.vbs.

## NAMESPACES.VBS

```
Dim fso
Dim l
Dim s


EnumNamespaces("root")

Sub EnumNamespaces(ByVal nspace)

Set ws = CreateObject("Wscript.Shell")
Set fso = CreateObject("Scripting.FilesystemObject")

If fso.folderExists(ws.currentDirectory & "\" & nspace) = false then
  fso.CreateFolder(ws.currentDirectory & "\" & nspace)
End If

On error Resume Next

Set objs = GetObject("Winmgmts:\\.\" &
nspace).InstancesOf("__Namespace", &H20000)

If err.Number <> 0 Then
  err.Clear
  Exit Sub
End If

For each obj in objs
```

```vbs
    EnumNamespaces(nspace & "\" & obj.Name)
Next

End Sub
```

## Categories.VBS

```vbs
Dim fso
Dim l
Dim s

Set ws = CreateObject("Wscript.Shell")
Set fso = CreateObject("Scripting.FilesystemObject")

EnumNamespaces("root")


Sub EnumNamespaces(ByVal nspace)

EnumCategories(nspace)

If fso.folderExists(ws.currentDirectory & "\" & nspace) = false then
 fso.CreateFolder(ws.currentDirectory & "\" & nspace)
End If

On error Resume Next

Set objs = GetObject("Winmgmts:\\.\" &
nspace).InstancesOf("___Namespace", &H20000)

If err.Number <> 0 Then
 err.Clear
 Exit Sub
```

```vbscript
   End If

   For each obj in objs

      EnumNamespaces(nspace & "\" & obj.Name)

   Next

End Sub

Sub EnumCategories(ByVal nspace)

Set ws = CreateObject("Wscript.Shell")
Set fso = CreateObject("Scripting.FilesystemObject")

Set objs = GetObject("Winmgmts:\\.\" & nspace).SubClassesOf("", &H20000)
For each obj in objs

   pos = instr(obj.Path_.class, "_")

   if pos = 0 then
      If fso.folderExists(ws.currentDirectory & "\" & nspace & "\" &
obj.Path_.Class) = false then
         fso.CreateFolder(ws.currentDirectory & "\" & nspace & "\" &
obj.Path_.Class)
      End If
   else
      if pos = 1 then
         If fso.folderExists(ws.currentDirectory & "\" & nspace &
"\SuperClasses") = false then
            fso.CreateFolder(ws.currentDirectory & "\" & nspace &
"\SuperClasses")
         End If
```

```
        else
            If fso.folderExists(ws.currentDirectory & "\" & nspace & "\" &
Mid(obj.Path_.Class, 1, pos-1)) = false then
                fso.CreateFolder(ws.currentDirectory & "\" & nspace & "\" &
Mid(obj.Path_.Class, 1, pos-1))
            End If
          End If
        End If


    Next


End Sub
```

## Classes.VBS

```
    Dim fso
    Dim l
    Dim s

    EnumNamespaces("root")

    Sub EnumNamespaces(ByVal nspace)

    EnumClasses(nspace)

    Set ws = CreateObject("Wscript.Shell")
    Set fso = CreateObject("Scripting.FilesystemObject")

    If fso.folderExists(ws.currentDirectory & "\" & nspace) = false then
     fso.CreateFolder(ws.currentDirectory & "\" & nspace)
    End If
```

```
On error Resume Next

Set objs = GetObject("Winmgmts:\\.\" &
nspace).InstancesOf("___Namespace", &H20000)

  If err.Number <> 0 Then
   err.Clear
   Exit Sub
  End If

For each obj in objs

    EnumNamespaces(nspace & "\" & obj.Name)

Next

End Sub

Sub EnumClasses(ByVal nspace)

Set ws = CreateObject("Wscript.Shell")
Set fso = CreateObject("Scripting.FilesystemObject")

Set objs = GetObject("Winmgmts:\\.\" & nspace).SubClassesOf("", &H20000)
For each obj in objs

    pos = instr(obj.Path_.class, "_")

    if pos = 0 then
        call CreateXMLFile(ws.CurrentDirectory & "\" & nspace & "\" &
obj.Path_.Class, nspace, obj.Path_.Class)
      else
       if pos = 1 then
```

```
        call CreateXMlFile(ws.CurrentDirectory & "\" & nspace &
"\Superclasses", nspace, obj.Path_.Class)
        else
        call CreateXMLFile(ws.CurrentDirectory & "\" & nspace & "\" &
Mid(obj.Path_.Class, 1, pos-1), nspace, obj.Path_.Class)
        End If
      End If


    Next


    End Sub


    Sub CreateXMLFile(ByVal Path, ByVal nspace, ByVal ClassName)



    Set fso = CreateObject("Scripting.FileSystemObject")
    Dim shorty
    On error Resume Next
    shorty = fso.GetFolder(Path).ShortPath
    If err.Number <> 0 then
    err.Clear
    Exit Sub
    End IF



    set obj = GetObject("Winmgmts:\\.\" & nspace).Get(classname)

    Set txtstream = fso.OpenTextFile(Shorty & "\" & Classname & ".xml", 2, true, -
2)
    txtstream.WriteLine("<data>")
    txtstream.WriteLine("  <NamespaceInformation>")
    txtstream.WriteLine("    <namespace>" & nspace & "</namespace>")
```

```
txtstream.WriteLine("   <classname>" & classname & "</classname>")
txtstream.WriteLine("  </NamespaceInformation>")
txtstream.WriteLine("  <properties>")

for each prop in obj.Properties_
    txtstream.WriteLine("   <property Name = """ & prop.Name & """
IsArray=""" & prop.IsArray & """ DataType = """ &
prop.Qualifiers_("CIMType").Value & """/>")
    Next
txtstream.WriteLine("  </properties>")
txtstream.WriteLine("</data>")
txtstream.close

End sub
```

As shown below, once these routines are done, you should be able to go to the folder, based on what I've told you about the Namespace\category\classes

Directory ▸ root ▸ CIMV2 ▸ Win32

| Name | Date modified | Type |
|------|---------------|------|
| ☆ Favorites | | |
| Desktop | | |
| Downloads | | |
| Recent places | | |
| Win32_1394Controller | 6/5/2018 6:41 PM | XML File |
| Win32_1394ControllerDevice | 6/5/2018 6:41 PM | XML File |
| Win32_Account | 6/5/2018 6:41 PM | XML File |
| Win32_AccountSID | 6/5/2018 6:41 PM | XML File |
| This PC | | |
| Win32_ACE | 6/5/2018 6:41 PM | XML File |
| Desktop | | |
| Win32_ActionCheck | 6/5/2018 6:42 PM | XML File |
| Documents | | |
| Win32_ActiveRoute | 6/5/2018 6:41 PM | XML File |
| Downloads | | |
| Win32_AllocatedResource | 6/5/2018 6:41 PM | XML File |
| Music | | |
| Win32_ApplicationCommandLine | 6/5/2018 6:41 PM | XML File |
| Pictures | | |
| Win32_ApplicationService | 6/5/2018 6:41 PM | XML File |
| Videos | | |
| Win32_AssociatedProcessorMemory | 6/5/2018 6:41 PM | XML File |
| Local Disk (C:) | | |
| Win32_AutochkSetting | 6/5/2018 6:41 PM | XML File |
| DVD RW Drive (D:) DN600ENU2 | | |
| Win32_BaseBoard | 6/5/2018 6:41 PM | XML File |
| Local Disk (E:) | | |
| Win32_BaseService | 6/5/2018 6:41 PM | XML File |
| Powershell Basic Examples (F:) | | |
| Win32_Battery | 6/5/2018 6:41 PM | XML File |
| New Volume (G:) | | |
| Win32_Binary | 6/5/2018 6:41 PM | XML File |
| New Volume (H:) | | |
| Win32_BindImageAction | 6/5/2018 6:41 PM | XML File |
| | Win32_BIOS | 6/5/2018 6:41 PM | XML File |
| Network | | |
| Win32_BootConfiguration | 6/5/2018 6:41 PM | XML File |
| WDMYCLOUD | | |
| Win32_Bus | 6/5/2018 6:41 PM | XML File |
| WDMYCLOUD1 | | |
| Win32_CacheMemory | 6/5/2018 6:41 PM | XML File |
| WIN-SJRLOAKMF5B | | |
| Win32_CDROMDrive | 6/5/2018 6:41 PM | XML File |
| WIN-VNQ7KUKQ4NE | | |
| Win32_CheckCheck | 6/5/2018 6:42 PM | XML File |
| | Win32_CIMLogicalDeviceCIMDataFile | 6/5/2018 6:41 PM | XML File |
| | Win32_ClassicCOMApplicationClasses | 6/5/2018 6:41 PM | XML File |

686 items

And If you open one of these up:

```xml
- <data>
  - <NamespaceInformation>
      <namespace>root\CIMV2</namespace>
      <classname>Win32_BIOS</classname>
    </NamespaceInformation>
  - <properties>
      <property Name="BiosCharacteristics" IsArray="True" DataType="uint16"/>
      <property Name="BIOSVersion" IsArray="True" DataType="string"/>
      <property Name="BuildNumber" IsArray="False" DataType="string"/>
      <property Name="Caption" IsArray="False" DataType="string"/>
      <property Name="CodeSet" IsArray="False" DataType="string"/>
      <property Name="CurrentLanguage" IsArray="False" DataType="string"/>
      <property Name="Description" IsArray="False" DataType="string"/>
      <property Name="IdentificationCode" IsArray="False" DataType="string"/>
      <property Name="InstallableLanguages" IsArray="False" DataType="uint16"/>
      <property Name="InstallDate" IsArray="False" DataType="datetime"/>
      <property Name="LanguageEdition" IsArray="False" DataType="string"/>
      <property Name="ListOfLanguages" IsArray="True" DataType="string"/>
      <property Name="Manufacturer" IsArray="False" DataType="string"/>
      <property Name="Name" IsArray="False" DataType="string"/>
      <property Name="OtherTargetOS" IsArray="False" DataType="string"/>
      <property Name="PrimaryBIOS" IsArray="False" DataType="boolean"/>
      <property Name="ReleaseDate" IsArray="False" DataType="datetime"/>
      <property Name="SerialNumber" IsArray="False" DataType="string"/>
      <property Name="SMBIOSBIOSVersion" IsArray="False" DataType="string"/>
      <property Name="SMBIOSMajorVersion" IsArray="False" DataType="uint16"/>
      <property Name="SMBIOSMinorVersion" IsArray="False" DataType="uint16"/>
      <property Name="SMBIOSPresent" IsArray="False" DataType="boolean"/>
      <property Name="SoftwareElementID" IsArray="False" DataType="string"/>
      <property Name="SoftwareElementState" IsArray="False" DataType="uint16"/>
      <property Name="Status" IsArray="False" DataType="string"/>
      <property Name="TargetOperatingSystem" IsArray="False" DataType="uint16"/>
      <property Name="Version" IsArray="False" DataType="string"/>
    </properties>
  </data>
```

# The Many ways to use your WMI skills and impress people

The following is list of the what we're going to be using with WMI:

ASP

ASPX

Attribute XML

Delimited Files

Element XML

Element XML For XSL

Excel

HTA

HTML

Schema XML

XSL

I need to do this before someone complains.

Up to here, the various languages I'm going to cover will have the same chapters. But past here, the code is specifically for each language. All will have the same code examples but written in the language specified in the title.

# Core Code

*Because it should only be written once or twice and maybe three times*

As I write this, I'm looking for the easiest way to get the task done and I'm realizing that, in fact, there are three ways to do it.

1.  Interleave the code into the output routines
2.  Use arrays to create a names collection and a column and rows collection
3.  Use the dictionary object to create a names collection, a columns collection and a rows collection.

Since I have 7 books here, I can use one of each for three books and do another three for the next set of three leaving one for anyone of the three.

With that said, let's me show you how each would work:

Below is the inline code:

```
function GetValue
{
   param
   (
   [string]$Name,
```

```
[object]$obj
)
[string]$PName = $Name + " = "
[string]$tempstr = $obj.GetObjectText_(0)
$pos = $tempstr.IndexOf($PName)
if ($pos -gt 0)
{
    $pos = $pos + $PName.Length
    $tempstr = $tempstr.SubString($pos, ($tempstr.Length - $pos))
    $pos = $tempstr.IndexOf(";")
    $tempstr = $tempstr.SubString(0, $pos)
    $tempstr = $tempstr.Replace('"', "")
    $tempstr = $tempstr.Replace("}", "")
    $tempstr = $tempstr.Replace("{", "")
    $tempstr = $tempstr.Trim()
    if($tempstr.Length -gt 14)
    {
        if($obj.Properties_.Item($Name).CIMType -eq 101)
        {
            [System.String]$tstr = $tempstr.SubString(4, 2)
            $tstr = $tstr + "/"
            $tstr = $tstr + $tempstr.SubString(6, 2)
            $tstr = $tstr + "/"
            $tstr = $tstr + $tempstr.SubString(0, 4)
            $tstr = $tstr + " "
            $tstr = $tstr + $tempstr.SubString(8, 2)
            $tstr = $tstr + ":"
            $tstr = $tstr + $tempstr.SubString(10, 2)
            $tstr = $tstr + ":"
            $tstr = $tstr + $tempstr.SubString(12, 2)
            $tempstr = $tstr
        }
    }
```

```
    return $tempstr
  }
  else
  {
    return ""
  }
}
$strQuery= "Select * From ___InstanceModificationEvent WITHIN 1 where
TargetInstance ISA 'Win32_Process'"

$ws = new-object -com WScript.Shell
$fso = new-object -com Scripting.FileSystemObject
$txtstream = $fso.OpenTextFile($ws.CurrentDirectory + "\Win32_Process.html", 2,
$true, -2)
$txtstream.WriteLine("<html>")
$txtstream.WriteLine("<head>")
$txtstream.WriteLine("<style type='text/css'>")
$txtstream.WriteLine("th")
$txtstream.WriteLine("{")
$txtstream.WriteLine("    COLOR: darkred;")
$txtstream.WriteLine("    BACKGROUND-COLOR: white;")
$txtstream.WriteLine("    FONT-FAMILY:font-family: Cambria, serif;")
$txtstream.WriteLine("    FONT-SIZE: 12px;")
$txtstream.WriteLine("    text-align: left;")
$txtstream.WriteLine("    white-Space: nowrap;")
$txtstream.WriteLine("}")
$txtstream.WriteLine("td")
$txtstream.WriteLine("{")
$txtstream.WriteLine("    COLOR: navy;")
$txtstream.WriteLine("    BACKGROUND-COLOR: white;")
$txtstream.WriteLine("    FONT-FAMILY: font-family: Cambria, serif;")
$txtstream.WriteLine("    FONT-SIZE: 12px;")
$txtstream.WriteLine("    text-align: left;")
```

```
$txtstream.WriteLine("   white-Space: nowrap;")
$txtstream.WriteLine("}")
$txtstream.WriteLine("</style>")
$txtstream.WriteLine("<title>Win32_Process</title>")
$txtstream.WriteLine("</head>")
$txtstream.WriteLine("<body>")
$txtstream.WriteLine("<table Border='1' cellpadding='3' cellspacing='3'>")

$Locale = "MS_0409"
$Authentication = 6
$Impersonation = 3
$iret = [reflection.assembly]::LoadWithPartialName("'Microsoft.VisualBasic")
$svc = [Microsoft.VisualBasic.Interaction]::GetObject("winmgmts:[locale=" +
$Locale + "]\\.\root\cimv2")
$svc.Security_.AuthenticationLevel = $Authentication
$svc.Security_.ImpersonationLevel= $Impersonation
$es = $svc.ExecNotificationQuery($strQuery)
While($v -lt 4)
{
    $ti = $es.NextEvent(-1)
    $obj = $ti.Properties_.Item("TargetInstance").Value
    if($v -eq 0)
    {
        $txtstream.WriteLine("<tr>")
        foreach($prop in $obj.Properties_)
        {
            $txtstream.WriteLine("<th>" + $prop.Name + "</th>")
        }
        $txtstream.WriteLine("</tr>")
        $txtstream.WriteLine("<tr>")
        foreach($prop in $obj.Properties_)
        {
            $Value = $GetValue $prop.Name $obj
```

```
        $txtstream.WriteLine("<td>" + $Value + "</td>")
    }
    $txtstream.WriteLine("</tr>")

}
Else
{
    $txtstream.WriteLine("<tr>")
    foreach($prop in $obj.Properties_)
    {
        $Value = $GetValue $prop.Name $obj
        $txtstream.WriteLine("<td>" + $Value + "</td>")
    }
    $txtstream.WriteLine("</tr>")

}
}
$txtstream.WriteLine("</table>")
$txtstream.WriteLine("</body>")
$txtstream.WriteLine("</html>")
$txtstream.Close()
```

Below is the Array code:

```
[Array]$Names
[Array]$Values

function GetValue
{
  param
  (
  [string]$Name,
  [object]$obj
  )
  [string]$PName = $Name + " = "
  [string]$tempstr = $obj.GetObjectText_(0)
  $pos = $tempstr.IndexOf($PName)
  if ($pos -gt 0)
  {
    $pos = $pos + $PName.Length
    $tempstr = $tempstr.SubString($pos, ($tempstr.Length - $pos))
    $pos = $tempstr.IndexOf(";")
    $tempstr = $tempstr.SubString(0, $pos)
    $tempstr = $tempstr.Replace('"', "")
    $tempstr = $tempstr.Replace("}", "")
    $tempstr = $tempstr.Replace("{", "")
    $tempstr = $tempstr.Trim()
    if($tempstr.Length -gt 14)
    {
      if($obj.Properties_.Item($Name).CIMType -eq 101)
      {
        [System.String]$tstr = $tempstr.SubString(4, 2)
```

```
        $tstr = $tstr + "/"
        $tstr = $tstr + $tempstr.SubString(6, 2)
        $tstr = $tstr + "/"
        $tstr = $tstr + $tempstr.SubString(0, 4)
        $tstr = $tstr + " "
        $tstr = $tstr + $tempstr.SubString(8, 2)
        $tstr = $tstr + ":"
        $tstr = $tstr + $tempstr.SubString(10, 2)
        $tstr = $tstr + ":"
        $tstr = $tstr + $tempstr.SubString(12, 2)
        $tempstr = $tstr
      }
    }
    return $tempstr
  }
  else
  {
    return ""
  }
}


$strQuery= "Select * From ___InstanceModificationEvent WITHIN 1 where
TargetInstance ISA 'Win32_Process'"


$v=0
$x=0
$Locale = "MS_0409"
$Authentication = 6
$Impersonation = 3
$iret = [reflection.assembly]::LoadWithPartialName("'Microsoft.VisualBasic")
```

```
$svc = [Microsoft.VisualBasic.Interaction]::GetObject("winmgmts:[locale=" +
$Locale + "]\\.\root\cimv2")
$svc.Security_.AuthenticationLevel = $Authentication
$svc.Security_.ImpersonationLevel= $Impersonation
$es = $svc.ExecNotificationQuery($strQuery)
While($v -lt 400)
{
    $ti = $es.NextEvent(-1)
    $obj = $ti.Properties_.Item("TargetInstance").Value

    If($v -eq 0)
    {
        $Names=[Array]::CreateInstance([String], $obj.Properties_.Count)
        $Values=[Array]::CreateInstance([String], 400, $obj.Properties_.Count)
        foreach($prop in $obj.Properties_)
        {
            $Names[$x] = $prop.Name
            $Value = GetValue $prop.Name $obj
            $Values[0, $x] = $Value
            $x=$x+1
        }
        $x = 0
    }
    else
    {
        foreach($prop in $obj.Properties_)
        {
            $Values[$v, $x] = GetValue $prop.Name $obj
            $x = $x +1
        }
        $x= 0
    }
    $v=$v+1
```

24

```
}
$a=0
$b=0

$ws = new-object -com WScript.Shell
$fso = new-object -com Scripting.FileSystemObject
$txtstream = $fso.OpenTextFile($ws.CurrentDirectory + "\Win32_Process.html", 2,
$true, -2)
$txtstream.WriteLine("<html>")
$txtstream.WriteLine("<head>")
$txtstream.WriteLine("<style type='text/css'>")
$txtstream.WriteLine("th")
$txtstream.WriteLine("{")
$txtstream.WriteLine("    COLOR: darkred;")
$txtstream.WriteLine("    BACKGROUND-COLOR: white;")
$txtstream.WriteLine("    FONT-FAMILY:font-family: Cambria, serif;")
$txtstream.WriteLine("    FONT-SIZE: 12px;")
$txtstream.WriteLine("    text-align: left;")
$txtstream.WriteLine("    white-Space: nowrap;")
$txtstream.WriteLine("}")
$txtstream.WriteLine("td")
$txtstream.WriteLine("{")
$txtstream.WriteLine("    COLOR: navy;")
$txtstream.WriteLine("    BACKGROUND-COLOR: white;")
$txtstream.WriteLine("    FONT-FAMILY: font-family: Cambria, serif;")
$txtstream.WriteLine("    FONT-SIZE: 12px;")
$txtstream.WriteLine("    text-align: left;")
$txtstream.WriteLine("    white-Space: nowrap;")
$txtstream.WriteLine("}")
$txtstream.WriteLine("</style>")
$txtstream.WriteLine("<title>Win32_Process</title>")
$txtstream.WriteLine("</head>")
$txtstream.WriteLine("<body>")
```

```
$txtstream.WriteLine("<table Border='1' cellpadding='3' cellspacing='3'>")
$txtstream.WriteLine("<tr>")
for($a=0; $a -lt $Names.GetLength(0); $a++)
{
   $txtstream.WriteLine("<th>" + $Names[$a] + "</th>")
}
$txtstream.WriteLine("</tr>")
for($b=0; $b -lt $Values.GetLength(0); $b++)
{
   $txtstream.WriteLine("<tr>")
   for($a=0; $a -lt $Names.GetLength(0); $a++)
   {
      $Value = $Values[$b, $a]
      $txtstream.WriteLine("<td>" + $Value + "</td>")
   }
   $txtstream.WriteLine("</tr>")
}
$txtstream.WriteLine("</table>")
$txtstream.WriteLine("</body>")
$txtstream.WriteLine("</html>")
$txtstream.Close()
```

The Dictionary code:

Below is the Array code:

```
[Array]$Names
[Array]$Values

function GetValue
{
   param
```

```
(
[string]$Name,
[object]$obj
)
[string]$PName = $Name + " = "
[string]$tempstr = $obj.GetObjectText_(0)
$pos = $tempstr.IndexOf($PName)
if ($pos -gt 0)
{
   $pos = $pos + $PName.Length
   $tempstr = $tempstr.SubString($pos, ($tempstr.Length - $pos))
   $pos = $tempstr.IndexOf(";")
   $tempstr = $tempstr.SubString(0, $pos)
   $tempstr = $tempstr.Replace('"', "")
   $tempstr = $tempstr.Replace("}", "")
   $tempstr = $tempstr.Replace("{", "")
   $tempstr = $tempstr.Trim()
   if($tempstr.Length -gt 14)
   {
      if($obj.Properties_.Item($Name).CIMType -eq 101)
      {
         [System.String]$tstr = $tempstr.SubString(4, 2)
         $tstr = $tstr + "/"
         $tstr = $tstr + $tempstr.SubString(6, 2)
         $tstr = $tstr + "/"
         $tstr = $tstr + $tempstr.SubString(0, 4)
         $tstr = $tstr + " "
         $tstr = $tstr + $tempstr.SubString(8, 2)
         $tstr = $tstr + ":"
         $tstr = $tstr + $tempstr.SubString(10, 2)
         $tstr = $tstr + ":"
         $tstr = $tstr + $tempstr.SubString(12, 2)
         $tempstr = $tstr
```

```
        }
      }
      return $tempstr
    }
    else
    {
      return ""
    }
}



$strQuery= "Select * From ___InstanceModificationEvent WITHIN 1 where
TargetInstance ISA 'Win32_Process'"



$v=0
$x=0
$Locale = "MS_0409"
$Authentication = 6
$Impersonation = 3
$iret = [reflection.assembly]::LoadWithPartialName("'Microsoft.VisualBasic")
$svc = [Microsoft.VisualBasic.Interaction]::GetObject("winmgmts:[locale=" +
$Locale + "]\\.\root\cimv2")
$svc.Security_.AuthenticationLevel = $Authentication
$svc.Security_.ImpersonationLevel= $Impersonation
$es = $svc.ExecNotificationQuery($strQuery)
While($v -lt 400)
{
    $ti = $es.NextEvent(-1)
    $obj = $ti.Properties_.Item("TargetInstance").Value

    If($v -eq 0)
    {
```

```
$Names=[Array]::CreateInstance([String], $obj.Properties_.Count)
$Values=[Array]::CreateInstance([String], 400, $obj.Properties_.Count)
foreach($prop in $obj.Properties_)
{
    $Names[$x] = $prop.Name
    $Value = GetValue $prop.Name $obj
    $Values[0, $x] = $Value
    $x=$x+1
}
$x = 0
}
else
{
    foreach($prop in $obj.Properties_)
    {
        $Values[$v, $x] = GetValue $prop.Name $obj
        $x = $x +1
    }
    $x= 0
}
$v=$v+1
}
$a=0
$b=0

$ws = new-object -com WScript.Shell
$fso = new-object -com Scripting.FileSystemObject
$txtstream = $fso.OpenTextFile($ws.CurrentDirectory +  "\Win32_Process.html", 2,
$true, -2)
$txtstream.WriteLine("<html>")
$txtstream.WriteLine("<head>")
$txtstream.WriteLine("<style type='text/css'>")
$txtstream.WriteLine("th")
```

```
$txtstream.WriteLine("{")
$txtstream.WriteLine("   COLOR: darkred;")
$txtstream.WriteLine("   BACKGROUND-COLOR: white;")
$txtstream.WriteLine("   FONT-FAMILY:font-family: Cambria, serif;")
$txtstream.WriteLine("   FONT-SIZE: 12px;")
$txtstream.WriteLine("   text-align: left;")
$txtstream.WriteLine("   white-Space: nowrap;")
$txtstream.WriteLine("}")
$txtstream.WriteLine("td")
$txtstream.WriteLine("{")
$txtstream.WriteLine("   COLOR: navy;")
$txtstream.WriteLine("   BACKGROUND-COLOR: white;")
$txtstream.WriteLine("   FONT-FAMILY: font-family: Cambria, serif;")
$txtstream.WriteLine("   FONT-SIZE: 12px;")
$txtstream.WriteLine("   text-align: left;")
$txtstream.WriteLine("   white-Space: nowrap;")
$txtstream.WriteLine("}")
$txtstream.WriteLine("</style>")
$txtstream.WriteLine("<title>Win32_Process</title>")
$txtstream.WriteLine("</head>")
$txtstream.WriteLine("<body>")
$txtstream.WriteLine("<table Border='1' cellpadding='3' cellspacing='3'>")
$txtstream.WriteLine("<tr>")
for($a=0; $a -lt $Names.GetLength(0); $a++)
{
   $txtstream.WriteLine("<th>" + $Names[$a] + "</th>")
}
$txtstream.WriteLine("</tr>")
for($b=0; $b -lt $Values.GetLength(0); $b++)
{
   $txtstream.WriteLine("<tr>")
   for($a=0; $a -lt $Names.GetLength(0); $a++)
   {
```

```
    $Value = $Values[$b, $a]
    $txtstream.WriteLine("<td>" + $Value + "</td>")
  }
  $txtstream.WriteLine("</tr>")
}
$txtstream.WriteLine("</table>")
$txtstream.WriteLine("</body>")
$txtstream.WriteLine("</html>")
$txtstream.Close()
```

# Working with ASP

*What you should know first*

I NEED TO SHARE SOMETHING IMPOTANT WITH YOU THAT I HAVE SEEN ASKED BY PROS OVER AND OVER AGAIN. THE FACT THAT THEY ARE ASKING IT SHOWS JUST HOW UNAWARE THEY ARE OF THIS IMPORTANT FACT. Anything you write inside a textstream is considered by the compiler to be a string and not code.

So, if I type:

For VBScript, VB, VBS, VB.Net, Python, Ruby:
```
$txtstream.WriteLine("Response.Write(""<tr>"" & vbcrlf) ")
```
For JavaScript, JScript:
```
$txtstream.WriteLine("Response.Write(""<tr>"" & vbcrlf) ")
```
For Kixtart:
```
$txtstream.WriteLine("Response.Write(""<tr>"" & vbcrlf) ")
```
For C#:
```
$txtstream.WriteLine("Response.Write(\"<tr>\" & vbcrlf) ")
```
For C. . :
```
txtstream.WriteLine("Response.Write(\"<tr>\" & vbcrlf) ")
```
For PowerShell:
```
$txtstream.WriteLine("Response.Write(""<tr>"" & vbcrlf) ")
```

For Rexx:

```
txtstream~WriteLine("Response.Write(""<tr>"" & vbcrlf) ")
```

For Borland C Builder:

```
txtstream.OLEFunction("WriteLine", OleVariant("Response.Write(""<tr>"" &
vbcrlf) ")
```

For Borland Delphi:

```
$txtstream.WriteLine('Response.Write(''<tr> '' & vbcrlf) ')
```

Aside from conforming to the compiler's expectations for single and double quotes, see any difference in the Response.Write("<tr>" & vbcrlf). It's because that part of the code is written to run as VBScript.

That also means any of the 14 languages listed could also create any of the other 14 languages. Hence, Programs that write programs. Below, is the code for ASP. The getValue function is in Appendix B.

## Using Arrays

Here's the other problem. ExecNotificationQuery is event driven. That means while we can control how many times the event gets fired, we can't know before the event is fired just how many properties were dealing with.

It makes a lot more sense to create two arrays and used them after we've created the arrays to drive the rendering of the code. To do that, we first need to know how many properties the class usually has and build the names and values from that. The only thing missing is the number of times the values will be called and since we are setting that in code, the names array will already be done and the Values array will be ready to be fed what it needs to render the code when the amount of times the array needs to be populated.

```
function GetValue{

    Param(
    [parameter(position=0)]
```

```
       $Name,
       [parameter(position=1)]
       $obj

       )
[string]$PName = $Name + " = "
$tempstr = $obj.GetObjectText_(0)
$pos = $tempstr.IndexOf($PName)
if ($pos -gt 0)
{
    $pos = $pos + $PName.Length
    $tempstr = $tempstr.SubString($pos, ($tempstr.Length - $pos))
    $pos = $tempstr.IndexOf(";")
    $tempstr = $tempstr.SubString(0, $pos)
    $tempstr = $tempstr.Replace("'", "")
    $tempstr = $tempstr.Replace("}", "")
    $tempstr = $tempstr.Replace("{", "")
    $tempstr = $tempstr.Trim()
    if($tempstr.Length -gt 14)
    {
        if($obj.Properties_.Item($Name).CIMType -eq 101)
        {
            [System.String]$tstr = $tempstr.SubString(4, 2)
            $tstr = $tstr + "/"
            $tstr = $tstr + $tempstr.SubString(6, 2)
            $tstr = $tstr + "/"
            $tstr = $tstr + $tempstr.SubString(0, 4)
            $tstr = $tstr + " "
            $tstr = $tstr + $tempstr.SubString(8, 2)
            $tstr = $tstr + ":"
            $tstr = $tstr + $tempstr.SubString(10, 2)
            $tstr = $tstr + ":"
            $tstr = $tstr + $tempstr.SubString(12, 2)
```

```
        $tempstr = $tstr
      }
    }
    return $tempstr
  }
  else
  {
    return ""
  }
}

[int]$y=0
[int]$x=0
[array]$names = $null
[array]$values = $null
$Locale = "MS_0409"
$Authentication = 6
$Impersonation = 3
$iret = [reflection.assembly]::LoadWithPartialName("'Microsoft.VisualBasic")
$svc = [Microsoft.VisualBasic.Interaction]::GetObject("winmgmts:[locale=" +
$Locale + "]\\.\root\cimv2")
$svc.Security_.AuthenticationLevel = $Authentication
$svc.Security_.ImpersonationLevel= $Impersonation
$strQuery= "Select * From ___InstanceModificationEvent WITHIN 1 where
TargetInstance ISA 'Win32_Process'"
$es = $svc.ExecNotificationQuery($strQuery)
while($y -lt 4)
{
  $ti = $es.NextEvent(-1)
  $obj = $ti.Properties_.Item("TargetInstance").Value
  if($y -eq 0)
  {
```

```
        $names = [array]::CreateInstance([System.String],
$obj.Properties_.Count)
        $values = [array]::CreateInstance([System.String], 4,
$obj.Properties_.Count)
      foreach($prop in $obj.Properties_)
      {
        $names[$x] = $prop.Name
        $values[$y, $x] = GetValue $prop.Name $obj
        $x=$x+1
      }
      $x=0
    }
    else
    {
      foreach($prop in $obj.Properties_)
      {
        $values[$y, $x] = GetValue $prop.Name $obj
        $x=$x+1
      }
      $x=0
    }
    $y=$y+1
  }




  $ws = New-object -com WScript.Shell
  $fso = New-Object -com Scripting.FileSystemObject
  $txtstream = $fso.OpenTextFile($ws.CurrentDirectory .
"\\Win32_Process.asp", 2, $true, -2)
```

## For Single Line Horizontal

```
$ws = New-object -com WScript.Shell
$fso = New-Object -com Scripting.FileSystemObject
$txtstream = $fso.OpenTextFile($ws.CurrentDirectory +
"\\Win32_Process.asp", 2, $true, -2)
$txtstream.WriteLine("<html>")
$txtstream.WriteLine("<head>")
$txtstream.WriteLine("<style type='text/css'>")
$txtstream.WriteLine("th")
$txtstream.WriteLine("{")
$txtstream.WriteLine("   COLOR: darkred;")
$txtstream.WriteLine("   BACKGROUND-COLOR: white;")
$txtstream.WriteLine("   FONT-FAMILY:font-family: Cambria, serif;")
$txtstream.WriteLine("   FONT-SIZE: 12px;")
$txtstream.WriteLine("   text-align: left;")
$txtstream.WriteLine("   white-Space: nowrap;")
$txtstream.WriteLine("}")
$txtstream.WriteLine("td")
$txtstream.WriteLine("{")
$txtstream.WriteLine("   COLOR: navy;")
$txtstream.WriteLine("   BACKGROUND-COLOR: white;")
$txtstream.WriteLine("   FONT-FAMILY: font-family: Cambria, serif;")
$txtstream.WriteLine("   FONT-SIZE: 12px;")
$txtstream.WriteLine("   text-align: left;")
$txtstream.WriteLine("   white-Space: nowrap;")
$txtstream.WriteLine("}")
$txtstream.WriteLine("</style>")
$txtstream.WriteLine("<title>Win32_Process</title>")
$txtstream.WriteLine("</head>")
$txtstream.WriteLine("<body>")
$txtstream.WriteLine("<table Border='1' cellpadding='1' cellspacing='1'>")
$txtstream.WriteLine("<%")
```

```
$txtstream.WriteLine("Response.Write(""<tr>"" & vbcrlf)")
for($x=0;$x -lt $names.GetLength(0)-1;$x++)
{
    $txtstream.WriteLine("Response.Write(""<th>" + $names[$x] + "</th>"" &
vbcrlf)")
}
$txtstream.WriteLine("Response.Write(""</tr>"" & vbcrlf)")
$txtstream.WriteLine("Response.Write(""<tr>"" & vbcrlf)")
for($x=0;$x -lt $names.GetLength(0)-1;$x++)
{
    [System.String]$value =$values[0, $x]
    $txtstream.WriteLine("Response.Write(""<td>" + $value + "</td>"" &
vbcrlf)")
}
$txtstream.WriteLine("Response.Write(""</tr>"" & vbcrlf)")
$txtstream.WriteLine("%>")
$txtstream.WriteLine("</table>")
$txtstream.WriteLine("</body>")
$txtstream.WriteLine("</html>")
$txtstream.Close()
```

## For Multi Line Horizontal

```
$ws = New-object -com WScript.Shell
$fso = New-Object -com Scripting.FileSystemObject
$txtstream = $fso.OpenTextFile($ws.CurrentDirectory +
"\\Win32_Process.asp", 2, $true, -2)
$txtstream.WriteLine("<html>")
$txtstream.WriteLine("<head>")
$txtstream.WriteLine("<style type='text/css'>")
$txtstream.WriteLine("th")
$txtstream.WriteLine("{")
$txtstream.WriteLine("    COLOR: darkred;")
```

```
$txtstream.WriteLine("   BACKGROUND-COLOR: white;")
$txtstream.WriteLine("   FONT-FAMILY:font-family: Cambria, serif;")
$txtstream.WriteLine("   FONT-SIZE: 12px;")
$txtstream.WriteLine("   text-align: left;")
$txtstream.WriteLine("   white-Space: nowrap;")
$txtstream.WriteLine("}")
$txtstream.WriteLine("td")
$txtstream.WriteLine("{“)
$txtstream.WriteLine("   COLOR: navy;")
$txtstream.WriteLine("   BACKGROUND-COLOR: white;")
$txtstream.WriteLine("   FONT-FAMILY: font-family: Cambria, serif;")
$txtstream.WriteLine("   FONT-SIZE: 12px;")
$txtstream.WriteLine("   text-align: left;")
$txtstream.WriteLine("   white-Space: nowrap;")
$txtstream.WriteLine("}")
$txtstream.WriteLine("</style>“)
$txtstream.WriteLine("<title>Win32_Process</title>“)
$txtstream.WriteLine("</head>“)
$txtstream.WriteLine("<body>“)
$txtstream.WriteLine("<table Border='1' cellpadding='1' cellspacing='1'>")
$txtstream.WriteLine("<%")
$txtstream.WriteLine("Response.Write(""<tr>"" & vbcrlf)")
for($x=0;$x -lt $names.GetLength(0)-1;$x++)
{
    $txtstream.WriteLine("Response.Write(""<th>" + $names[$x] + "</th>"" &
vbcrlf)")
}
$txtstream.WriteLine("Response.Write(""</tr>"" & vbcrlf)")
for($y=0;$y -lt $values.GetLength(0)-1;$y++)
{
    $txtstream.WriteLine("Response.Write(""<tr>"" & vbcrlf)")
    for($x=0;$x -lt $names.GetLength(0)-1;$x++)
    {
```

39

```
        [System.String]$value =$values[$y, $x]
        $txtstream.WriteLine("Response.Write(""<td>" + $value + "</td>""" &
vbcrlf)")
      }
      $txtstream.WriteLine("Response.Write(""</tr>""" & vbcrlf)")
    }
    $txtstream.WriteLine("%>")
    $txtstream.WriteLine("</table>")
    $txtstream.WriteLine("</body>")
    $txtstream.WriteLine("</html>")
    $txtstream.Close()
```

## For Single Line Vertical

```
$ws = New-object -com WScript.Shell
$fso = New-Object -com Scripting.FileSystemObject
$txtstream = $fso.OpenTextFile($ws.CurrentDirectory +
"\\Win32_Process.asp", 2, $true, -2)
$txtstream.WriteLine("<html>")
$txtstream.WriteLine("<head>")
$txtstream.WriteLine("<style type='text/css'>")
$txtstream.WriteLine("th")
$txtstream.WriteLine("{")
$txtstream.WriteLine("   COLOR: darkred;")
$txtstream.WriteLine("   BACKGROUND-COLOR: white;")
$txtstream.WriteLine("   FONT-FAMILY:font-family: Cambria, serif;")
$txtstream.WriteLine("   FONT-SIZE: 12px;")
$txtstream.WriteLine("   text-align: left;")
$txtstream.WriteLine("   white-Space: nowrap;")
$txtstream.WriteLine("}")
$txtstream.WriteLine("td")
$txtstream.WriteLine("{")
$txtstream.WriteLine("   COLOR: navy;")
$txtstream.WriteLine("   BACKGROUND-COLOR: white;")
```

```
$txtstream.WriteLine("   FONT-FAMILY: font-family: Cambria, serif;")
$txtstream.WriteLine("   FONT-SIZE: 12px;")
$txtstream.WriteLine("   text-align: left;")
$txtstream.WriteLine("   white-Space: nowrap;")
$txtstream.WriteLine("}")
$txtstream.WriteLine("</style>")
$txtstream.WriteLine("<title>Win32_Process</title>")
$txtstream.WriteLine("</head>")
$txtstream.WriteLine("<body>")
$txtstream.WriteLine("<table Border='1' cellpadding='1' cellspacing='1'>")
$txtstream.WriteLine("<%")
$txtstream.WriteLine("Response.Write(""<tr>"" & vbcrlf)")
for($x=0;$x -lt $names.GetLength(0)-1;$x++)
{
    [System.String]$value =$values[0, $x]
    $txtstream.WriteLine("Response.Write(""<tr><th>" + $names[$x] +
"</th><td>" + $value + "</td></tr>"" & vbcrlf)")
    }
}
$txtstream.WriteLine("%>")
$txtstream.WriteLine("</table>")
$txtstream.WriteLine("</body>")
$txtstream.WriteLine("</html>")
$txtstream.Close()
```

For Multi Line Vertical

```
$ws = New-object -com WScript.Shell
$fso = New-Object -com Scripting.FileSystemObject
$txtstream = $fso.OpenTextFile($ws.CurrentDirectory +
"\\Win32_Process.asp", 2, $true, -2)
$txtstream.WriteLine("<html>")
```

```
$txtstream.WriteLine("<head>")
$txtstream.WriteLine("<style type='text/css'>")
$txtstream.WriteLine("th")
$txtstream.WriteLine("{")
$txtstream.WriteLine("    COLOR: darkred;")
$txtstream.WriteLine("    BACKGROUND-COLOR: white;")
$txtstream.WriteLine("    FONT-FAMILY:font-family: Cambria, serif;")
$txtstream.WriteLine("    FONT-SIZE: 12px;")
$txtstream.WriteLine("    text-align: left;")
$txtstream.WriteLine("    white-Space: nowrap;")
$txtstream.WriteLine("}")
$txtstream.WriteLine("td")
$txtstream.WriteLine("{")
$txtstream.WriteLine("    COLOR: navy;")
$txtstream.WriteLine("    BACKGROUND-COLOR: white;")
$txtstream.WriteLine("    FONT-FAMILY: font-family: Cambria, serif;")
$txtstream.WriteLine("    FONT-SIZE: 12px;")
$txtstream.WriteLine("    text-align: left;")
$txtstream.WriteLine("    white-Space: nowrap;")
$txtstream.WriteLine("}")
$txtstream.WriteLine("</style>")
$txtstream.WriteLine("<title>Win32_Process</title>")
$txtstream.WriteLine("</head>")
$txtstream.WriteLine("<body>")
$txtstream.WriteLine("<table Border='1' cellpadding='1' cellspacing='1'>")
$txtstream.WriteLine("<%")
for($x=0;$x -lt $names.GetLength(0)-1;$x++)
{
    $txtstream.WriteLine("Response.Write(""<tr><th>" + $names[$x] +
"</th>"" & vbcrlf)")
}
for($y=0;$y -lt $values.GetLength(0)-1;$y++)
{
```

42

```
            [System.String]$value =$values[$y, $x]
            $txtstream.WriteLine("Response.Write(""<td>" + $value + "</td>""" &
vbcrlf)")
        }
        $txtstream.WriteLine("Response.Write(""</tr>""" & vbcrlf)")
    }
    $txtstream.WriteLine("%>")
    $txtstream.WriteLine("</table>")
    $txtstream.WriteLine("</body>")
    $txtstream.WriteLine("</html>")
    $txtstream.Close()
```

# ASPX Code

B elow, is the code for ASP. The getValue function is in Appendix B.

```
function GetValue{

    Param(
    [parameter(position=0)]
    $Name,
    [parameter(position=1)]
    $obj

    )
    [string]$PName = $Name + " = "
    $tempstr = $obj.GetObjectText_(0)
    $pos = $tempstr.IndexOf($PName)
    if ($pos -gt 0)
    {
        $pos = $pos + $PName.Length
        $tempstr = $tempstr.SubString($pos, ($tempstr.Length - $pos))
        $pos = $tempstr.IndexOf(";")
        $tempstr = $tempstr.SubString(0, $pos)
        $tempstr = $tempstr.Replace('"', "")
```

```
     $tempstr = $tempstr.Replace("}", "")
     $tempstr = $tempstr.Replace("{", "")
     $tempstr = $tempstr.Trim()
     if($tempstr.Length -gt 14)
     {
        if($obj.Properties_.Item($Name).CIMType -eq 101)
        {
           [System.String]$tstr = $tempstr.SubString(4, 2)
           $tstr = $tstr + "/"
           $tstr = $tstr + $tempstr.SubString(6, 2)
           $tstr = $tstr + "/"
           $tstr = $tstr + $tempstr.SubString(0, 4)
           $tstr = $tstr + " "
           $tstr = $tstr + $tempstr.SubString(8, 2)
           $tstr = $tstr + ":"
           $tstr = $tstr + $tempstr.SubString(10, 2)
           $tstr = $tstr + ":"
           $tstr = $tstr + $tempstr.SubString(12, 2)
           $tempstr = $tstr
        }
     }
     return $tempstr
   }
   else
   {
      return ""
   }
}

[int]$y=0
[int]$x=0
[array]$names = $null
[array]$values = $null
```

```
$Locale = "MS_0409"
$Authentication = 6
$Impersonation = 3
$iret = [reflection.assembly]::LoadWithPartialName("'Microsoft.VisualBasic")
$svc = [Microsoft.VisualBasic.Interaction]::GetObject("winmgmts:[locale=" +
$Locale + "]\\.\root\cimv2")
$svc.Security_.AuthenticationLevel = $Authentication
$svc.Security_.ImpersonationLevel= $Impersonation
$strQuery= "Select * From ___InstanceModificationEvent WITHIN 1 where
TargetInstance ISA 'Win32_Process'"
$es = $svc.ExecNotificationQuery($strQuery)
while($y -lt 4)
{
    $ti = $es.NextEvent(-1)
    $obj = $ti.Properties_.Item("TargetInstance").Value
    if($y -eq 0)
    {

        $names = [array]::CreateInstance([System.String],
$obj.Properties_.Count)
        $values = [array]::CreateInstance([System.String], 4,
$obj.Properties_.Count)
        foreach($prop in $obj.Properties_)
        {
          $names[$x] = $prop.Name
          $values[$y, $x] = GetValue $prop.Name $obj
          $x=$x+1
        }
        $x=0
    }
    else
    {
        foreach($prop in $obj.Properties_)
```

```
        {
          $values[$y, $x] = GetValue $prop.Name $obj
          $x=$x+1
        }
        $x=0
      }
      $y=$y+1
    }


    $ws = New-object -com WScript.Shell
    $fso = New-Object -com Scripting.FileSystemObject
    $txtstream = $fso.OpenTextFile($ws.CurrentDirectory +
"\Win32_Process.aspx", 2, $true, -2)
    $txtstream.WriteLine("<!DOCTYPE html PUBLIC ""-//W3C//DTD XHTML 1.0
Transitional//EN"" ""http://www.w3.org/TR/xhtml1/DTD/xhtml1-
transitional.dtd"">")
    $txtstream.WriteLine("")
    $txtstream.WriteLine("<html xmlns="http://www.w3.org/1999/xhtml"
>")
```

For Single Line Horizontal

```
    $txtstream.WriteLine("<head>")
    $txtstream.WriteLine("<style type='text/css'>")
    $txtstream.WriteLine("th")
    $txtstream.WriteLine("{")
    $txtstream.WriteLine("   COLOR: darkred;")
    $txtstream.WriteLine("   BACKGROUND-COLOR: white;")
    $txtstream.WriteLine("   FONT-FAMILY:font-family: Cambria, serif;")
    $txtstream.WriteLine("   FONT-SIZE: 12px;")
    $txtstream.WriteLine("   text-align: left;")
    $txtstream.WriteLine("   white-Space: nowrap;")
    $txtstream.WriteLine("}")
    $txtstream.WriteLine("td")
    $txtstream.WriteLine("{")
```

```
$txtstream.WriteLine("    COLOR: navy;")
$txtstream.WriteLine("    BACKGROUND-COLOR: white;")
$txtstream.WriteLine("    FONT-FAMILY: font-family: Cambria, serif;")
$txtstream.WriteLine("    FONT-SIZE: 12px;")
$txtstream.WriteLine("    text-align: left;")
$txtstream.WriteLine("    white-Space: nowrap;")
$txtstream.WriteLine("}")
$txtstream.WriteLine("</style>")
$txtstream.WriteLine("<title>Win32_Process</title>")
$txtstream.WriteLine("</head>")
$txtstream.WriteLine("<body>")
$txtstream.WriteLine("<table Border='1' cellpadding='1' cellspacing='1'>")
$txtstream.WriteLine("<%")
$txtstream.WriteLine("Response.Write(""<tr>"" & vbcrlf)")
for($x=0;$x -lt $names.GetLength(0)-1;$x++)
{
    $txtstream.WriteLine("Response.Write(""<th>" + $names[$x] + "</th>"" &
vbcrlf)")
}
$txtstream.WriteLine("Response.Write(""</tr>"" & vbcrlf)")
$txtstream.WriteLine("Response.Write(""<tr>"" & vbcrlf)")
for($x=0;$x -lt $names.GetLength(0)-1;$x++)
{
    [System.String]$value =$values[0, $x]
    $txtstream.WriteLine("Response.Write(""<td>" + $value + "</td>"" &
vbcrlf)")
}
$txtstream.WriteLine("Response.Write(""</tr>"" & vbcrlf)")
$txtstream.WriteLine("%>")
$txtstream.WriteLine("</table>")
$txtstream.WriteLine("</body>")
$txtstream.WriteLine("</html>")
$txtstream.Close()
```

## For Multi Line Horizontal

```
$txtstream.WriteLine("<head>")
$txtstream.WriteLine("<style type='text/css'>")
$txtstream.WriteLine("th")
$txtstream.WriteLine("{")
$txtstream.WriteLine("   COLOR: darkred;")
$txtstream.WriteLine("   BACKGROUND-COLOR: white;")
$txtstream.WriteLine("   FONT-FAMILY:font-family: Cambria, serif;")
$txtstream.WriteLine("   FONT-SIZE: 12px;")
$txtstream.WriteLine("   text-align: left;")
$txtstream.WriteLine("   white-Space: nowrap;")
$txtstream.WriteLine("}")
$txtstream.WriteLine("td")
$txtstream.WriteLine("{")
$txtstream.WriteLine("   COLOR: navy;")
$txtstream.WriteLine("   BACKGROUND-COLOR: white;")
$txtstream.WriteLine("   FONT-FAMILY: font-family: Cambria, serif;")
$txtstream.WriteLine("   FONT-SIZE: 12px;")
$txtstream.WriteLine("   text-align: left;")
$txtstream.WriteLine("   white-Space: nowrap;")
$txtstream.WriteLine("}")
$txtstream.WriteLine("</style>")
$txtstream.WriteLine("<title>Win32_Process</title>")
$txtstream.WriteLine("</head>")
$txtstream.WriteLine("<body>")
$txtstream.WriteLine("<table Border='1' cellpadding='1' cellspacing='1'>")
$txtstream.WriteLine("<%")
$txtstream.WriteLine("Response.Write(""<tr>"" & vbcrlf)")
for($x=0;$x -lt $names.GetLength(0)-1;$x++)
{
```

```
      $txtstream.WriteLine("Response.Write(""<th>" + $names[$x] + "</th>""" &
vbcrlf)")
   }
   $txtstream.WriteLine("Response.Write(""</tr>""" & vbcrlf)")
   for($y=0;$y -lt $values.GetLength(0)-1;$y++)
   {
      $txtstream.WriteLine("Response.Write(""<tr>""" & vbcrlf)")
      for($x=0;$x -lt $names.GetLength(0)-1;$x++)
      {
         [System.String]$value =$values[$y, $x]
         $txtstream.WriteLine("Response.Write(""<td>" + $value + "</td>""" &
vbcrlf)")
      }
      $txtstream.WriteLine("Response.Write(""</tr>""" & vbcrlf)")
   }
   $txtstream.WriteLine("%>")
   $txtstream.WriteLine("</table>")
   $txtstream.WriteLine("</body>")
   $txtstream.WriteLine("</html>")
   $txtstream.Close()
```

For Single Line Vertical

```
   $txtstream.WriteLine("<head>")
   $txtstream.WriteLine("<style type='text/css'>")
   $txtstream.WriteLine("th")
   $txtstream.WriteLine("{")
   $txtstream.WriteLine("   COLOR: darkred;")
   $txtstream.WriteLine("   BACKGROUND-COLOR: white;")
   $txtstream.WriteLine("   FONT-FAMILY:font-family: Cambria, serif;")
   $txtstream.WriteLine("   FONT-SIZE: 12px;")
   $txtstream.WriteLine("   text-align: left;")
   $txtstream.WriteLine("   white-Space: nowrap;")
   $txtstream.WriteLine("}")
```

```
$txtstream.WriteLine("td")
$txtstream.WriteLine("{")
$txtstream.WriteLine("    COLOR: navy;")
$txtstream.WriteLine("    BACKGROUND-COLOR: white;")
$txtstream.WriteLine("    FONT-FAMILY: font-family: Cambria, serif;")
$txtstream.WriteLine("    FONT-SIZE: 12px;")
$txtstream.WriteLine("    text-align: left;")
$txtstream.WriteLine("    white-Space: nowrap;")
$txtstream.WriteLine("}")
$txtstream.WriteLine("</style>")
$txtstream.WriteLine("<title>Win32_Process</title>")
$txtstream.WriteLine("</head>")
$txtstream.WriteLine("<body>")
$txtstream.WriteLine("<table Border='1' cellpadding='1' cellspacing='1'>")
$txtstream.WriteLine("<%")
$txtstream.WriteLine("Response.Write(""<tr>"" & vbcrlf)")
for($x=0;$x -lt $names.GetLength(0)-1;$x++)
{
    [System.String]$value =$values[0, $x]
    $txtstream.WriteLine("Response.Write(""<tr><th>" + $names[$x] +
"</th><td>" + $value + "</td></tr>"" & vbcrlf)")
    }
}
$txtstream.WriteLine("%>")
$txtstream.WriteLine("</table>")
$txtstream.WriteLine("</body>")
$txtstream.WriteLine("</html>")
$txtstream.Close()
```

For Multi Line Vertical

```
$txtstream.WriteLine("<head>")
$txtstream.WriteLine("<style type='text/css'>")
```

```
$txtstream.WriteLine("th")
$txtstream.WriteLine("{")
$txtstream.WriteLine("   COLOR: darkred;")
$txtstream.WriteLine("   BACKGROUND-COLOR: white;")
$txtstream.WriteLine("   FONT-FAMILY:font-family: Cambria, serif;")
$txtstream.WriteLine("   FONT-SIZE: 12px;")
$txtstream.WriteLine("   text-align: left;")
$txtstream.WriteLine("   white-Space: nowrap;")
$txtstream.WriteLine("}")
$txtstream.WriteLine("td")
$txtstream.WriteLine("{")
$txtstream.WriteLine("   COLOR: navy;")
$txtstream.WriteLine("   BACKGROUND-COLOR: white;")
$txtstream.WriteLine("   FONT-FAMILY: font-family: Cambria, serif;")
$txtstream.WriteLine("   FONT-SIZE: 12px;")
$txtstream.WriteLine("   text-align: left;")
$txtstream.WriteLine("   white-Space: nowrap;")
$txtstream.WriteLine("}")
$txtstream.WriteLine("</style>")
$txtstream.WriteLine("<title>Win32_Process</title>")
$txtstream.WriteLine("</head>")
$txtstream.WriteLine("<body>")
$txtstream.WriteLine("<table Border='1' cellpadding='1' cellspacing='1'>")
$txtstream.WriteLine("<%")
for($x=0;$x -lt $names.GetLength(0)-1;$x++)
{
    $txtstream.WriteLine("Response.Write(""<tr><th>" + $names[$x] +
"</th>""" & vbcrlf)")
}
for($y=0;$y -lt $values.GetLength(0)-1;$y++)
{
    [System.String]$value =$values[$y, $x]
```

```
        $txtstream.WriteLine("Response.Write(""<td>" + $value + "</td>""" &
vbcrlf)")
    }
    $txtstream.WriteLine("Response.Write(""</tr>""" & vbcrlf)")
}
$txtstream.WriteLine("%>")
$txtstream.WriteLine("</table>")
$txtstream.WriteLine("</body>")
$txtstream.WriteLine("</html>")
$txtstream.Close()
```

# HTA Code

Below, is the code for HTA. The getValue function is in Appendix B.

## Top Code

```
function GetValue{

    Param(
    [parameter(position=0)]
    $Name,
    [parameter(position=1)]
    $obj

    )
    [string]$PName = $Name + " = "
    $tempstr = $obj.GetObjectText_(0)
    $pos = $tempstr.IndexOf($PName)
    if ($pos -gt 0)
    {
        $pos = $pos + $PName.Length
```

```
$tempstr = $tempstr.SubString($pos, ($tempstr.Length - $pos))
$pos = $tempstr.IndexOf(";")
$tempstr = $tempstr.SubString(0, $pos)
$tempstr = $tempstr.Replace("'", "")
$tempstr = $tempstr.Replace("}", "")
$tempstr = $tempstr.Replace("{", "")
$tempstr = $tempstr.Trim()
if($tempstr.Length -gt 14)
{
   if($obj.Properties_.Item($Name).CIMType -eq 101)
   {
      [System.String]$tstr = $tempstr.SubString(4, 2)
      $tstr = $tstr + "/"
      $tstr = $tstr + $tempstr.SubString(6, 2)
      $tstr = $tstr + "/"
      $tstr = $tstr + $tempstr.SubString(0, 4)
      $tstr = $tstr + " "
      $tstr = $tstr + $tempstr.SubString(8, 2)
      $tstr = $tstr + ":"
      $tstr = $tstr + $tempstr.SubString(10, 2)
      $tstr = $tstr + ":"
      $tstr = $tstr + $tempstr.SubString(12, 2)
      $tempstr = $tstr
   }
}
return $tempstr
}
else
{
   return ""
}
}
```

```
[int]$y=0
[int]$x=0
[array]$names = $null
[array]$values = $null
$Locale = "MS_0409"
$Authentication = 6
$Impersonation = 3
$iret = [reflection.assembly]::LoadWithPartialName("'Microsoft.VisualBasic")
$svc = [Microsoft.VisualBasic.Interaction]::GetObject("winmgmts:[locale=" +
$Locale + "]\\.\root\cimv2")
$svc.Security_.AuthenticationLevel = $Authentication
$svc.Security_.ImpersonationLevel= $Impersonation
$strQuery= "Select * From ___InstanceModificationEvent WITHIN 1 where
TargetInstance ISA 'Win32_Process'"
$es = $svc.ExecNotificationQuery($strQuery)
while($y -lt 4)
{
   $ti = $es.NextEvent(-1)
   $obj = $ti.Properties_.Item("TargetInstance").Value
   if($y -eq 0)
   {

      $names = [array]::CreateInstance([System.String],
$obj.Properties_.Count)
      $values = [array]::CreateInstance([System.String], 4,
$obj.Properties_.Count)
      foreach($prop in $obj.Properties_)
      {
       $names[$x] = $prop.Name
       $values[$y, $x] = GetValue $prop.Name $obj
       $x=$x+1
      }
      $x=0
```

```
        }
        else
        {
          foreach($prop in $obj.Properties_)
          {
           $values[$y, $x] = GetValue $prop.Name $obj
           $x=$x+1
          }
          $x=0
        }
        $y=$y+1
      }
      $ws = New-object -com WScript.Shell
      $fso = New-Object -com Scripting.FileSystemObject
      $txtstream = $fso.OpenTextFile($ws.CurrentDirectory +
"\\Win32_Process.hta", 2, $true, -2)
      $txtstream.WriteLine("<html>")
      $txtstream.WriteLine("<head>")
      $txtstream.WriteLine("<HTA:APPLICATION ")
      $txtstream.WriteLine("ID = ""Process"" ")
      $txtstream.WriteLine("APPLICATIONNAME = ""Process"" ")
      $txtstream.WriteLine("SCROLL = ""yes"" ")
      $txtstream.WriteLine("SINGLEINSTANCE = ""yes"" ")
      $txtstream.WriteLine("WINDOWSTATE = ""maximize"" >")
      $txtstream.WriteLine("<title>Win32_Process</title>")
      $txtstream.WriteLine("<style type='text/css'>")
      $txtstream.WriteLine("th")
      $txtstream.WriteLine("{")
      $txtstream.WriteLine("   COLOR: darkred;")
      $txtstream.WriteLine("   BACKGROUND-COLOR: white;")
      $txtstream.WriteLine("   FONT-FAMILY:font-family: Cambria, serif;")
      $txtstream.WriteLine("   FONT-SIZE: 12px;")
      $txtstream.WriteLine("   text-align: left;")
```

```
$txtstream.WriteLine("   white-Space: nowrap;")
$txtstream.WriteLine("}")
$txtstream.WriteLine("td")
$txtstream.WriteLine("{“)
$txtstream.WriteLine("   COLOR: navy;")
$txtstream.WriteLine("   BACKGROUND-COLOR: white;")
$txtstream.WriteLine("   FONT-FAMILY: font-family: Cambria, serif;")
$txtstream.WriteLine("   FONT-SIZE: 12px;")
$txtstream.WriteLine("   text-align: left;")
$txtstream.WriteLine("   white-Space: nowrap;")
$txtstream.WriteLine("}")
$txtstream.WriteLine("</style>“)
$txtstream.WriteLine("</head>“)
$txtstream.WriteLine("<body>“)
#Use this if you want to create a border around your table:
$txtstream.WriteLine("<table Border='0' cellpadding='1' cellspacing='1'>“)

#Use this if you don't want to create a border around your table:
$txtstream.WriteLine("<table Border='1' cellpadding='1' cellspacing='1'>")
```

## For Single Line Horizontal

```
$txtstream.WriteLine("<tr>")
for($x=0;$x -lt $names.GetLength(0)-1;$x++)
{
    $txtstream.WriteLine("<th>" + $names[$x] + "</th>")
}
$txtstream.WriteLine("</tr>")
$txtstream.WriteLine("<tr>")
for($x=0;$x -lt $names.GetLength(0)-1;$x++)
{
    [System.String]$value =$values[0, $x]
    $txtstream.WriteLine("<td>" + $value + "</td>")
```

```
}
$txtstream.WriteLine("</tr>")
```

## For Multi Line Horizontal

```
$txtstream.WriteLine("<head>")
$txtstream.WriteLine("<style type='text/css'>")
$txtstream.WriteLine("th")
$txtstream.WriteLine("{")
$txtstream.WriteLine("   COLOR: darkred;")
$txtstream.WriteLine("   BACKGROUND-COLOR: white;")
$txtstream.WriteLine("   FONT-FAMILY:font-family: Cambria, serif;")
$txtstream.WriteLine("   FONT-SIZE: 12px;")
$txtstream.WriteLine("   text-align: left;")
$txtstream.WriteLine("   white-Space: nowrap;")
$txtstream.WriteLine("}")
$txtstream.WriteLine("td")
$txtstream.WriteLine("{")
$txtstream.WriteLine("   COLOR: navy;")
$txtstream.WriteLine("   BACKGROUND-COLOR: white;")
$txtstream.WriteLine("   FONT-FAMILY: font-family: Cambria, serif;")
$txtstream.WriteLine("   FONT-SIZE: 12px;")
$txtstream.WriteLine("   text-align: left;")
$txtstream.WriteLine("   white-Space: nowrap;")
$txtstream.WriteLine("}")
$txtstream.WriteLine("</style>")
$txtstream.WriteLine("<title>Win32_Process</title>")
$txtstream.WriteLine("</head>")
$txtstream.WriteLine("<body>")
$txtstream.WriteLine("<table Border='1' cellpadding='1' cellspacing='1'>")

$txtstream.WriteLine("<tr>")
for($x=0;$x -lt $names.GetLength(0)-1;$x++)
```

```
    {
        $txtstream.WriteLine("<th>" + $names[$x] + "</th>")
    }
    $txtstream.WriteLine("</tr>")
    for($y=0;$y -lt $values.GetLength(0)-1;$y++)
    {
        $txtstream.WriteLine("<tr>")
        for($x=0;$x -lt $names.GetLength(0)-1;$x++)
        {
            [System.String]$value =$values[$y, $x]
            $txtstream.WriteLine("<td>" + $value + "</td>")
        }
        $txtstream.WriteLine("</tr>")
    }
```

## For Single Line Vertical

```
$txtstream.WriteLine("<tr>")
for($x=0;$x -lt $names.GetLength(0)-1;$x++)
{
    [System.String]$value =$values[0, $x]
    $txtstream.WriteLine("<tr><th>" + $names[$x] + "</th><td>" + $value +
"</td></tr>")
    }
}
```

## For Multi Line Vertical

```
$txtstream.WriteLine("<table Border='1' cellpadding='1' cellspacing='1'>")

for($x=0;$x -lt $names.GetLength(0)-1;$x++)
{
    $txtstream.WriteLine("<tr><th>" + $names[$x] + "</th>")
```

```
}
for($y=0;$y –lt $values.GetLength(0)-1;$y++)
{
    [System.String]$value =$values[$y, $x]
    $txtstream.WriteLine("<td>" + $value + "</td>")
  }
  $txtstream.WriteLine("</tr>")
}
```

## End Code

```
$txtstream.WriteLine("</table>")
$txtstream.WriteLine("</body>")
$txtstream.WriteLine("</html>")
$txtstream.Close()
```

# HTML Code

B elow, is the code for HTML. The getValue function is in Appendix B.

## Top Code

```
function GetValue{

    Param(
    [parameter(position=0)]
    $Name,
    [parameter(position=1)]
    $obj

    )
[string]$PName = $Name + " = "
$tempstr = $obj.GetObjectText_(0)
$pos = $tempstr.IndexOf($PName)
if ($pos -gt 0)
{
    $pos = $pos + $PName.Length
    $tempstr = $tempstr.SubString($pos, ($tempstr.Length - $pos))
```

```
$pos = $tempstr.IndexOf(";")
$tempstr = $tempstr.SubString(0, $pos)
$tempstr = $tempstr.Replace("'", "")
$tempstr = $tempstr.Replace("}", "")
$tempstr = $tempstr.Replace("{", "")
$tempstr = $tempstr.Trim()
if($tempstr.Length -gt 14)
{
   if($obj.Properties_.Item($Name).CIMType -eq 101)
   {
      [System.String]$tstr = $tempstr.SubString(4, 2)
      $tstr = $tstr + "/"
      $tstr = $tstr + $tempstr.SubString(6, 2)
      $tstr = $tstr + "/"
      $tstr = $tstr + $tempstr.SubString(0, 4)
      $tstr = $tstr + " "
      $tstr = $tstr + $tempstr.SubString(8, 2)
      $tstr = $tstr + ":"
      $tstr = $tstr + $tempstr.SubString(10, 2)
      $tstr = $tstr + ":"
      $tstr = $tstr + $tempstr.SubString(12, 2)
      $tempstr = $tstr
   }
}
return $tempstr
}
else
{
   return ""
}
}

[int]$y=0
```

```powershell
[int]$x=0
[array]$names = $null
[array]$values = $null
$Locale = "MS_0409"
$Authentication = 6
$Impersonation = 3
$iret = [reflection.assembly]::LoadWithPartialName("'Microsoft.VisualBasic")
$svc = [Microsoft.VisualBasic.Interaction]::GetObject("winmgmts:[locale=" +
$Locale + "]\\.\root\cimv2")
$svc.Security_.AuthenticationLevel = $Authentication
$svc.Security_.ImpersonationLevel= $Impersonation
$strQuery= "Select * From ___InstanceModificationEvent WITHIN 1 where
TargetInstance ISA 'Win32_Process'"
$es = $svc.ExecNotificationQuery($strQuery)
while($y -lt 4)
{
    $ti = $es.NextEvent(-1)
    $obj = $ti.Properties_.Item("TargetInstance").Value
    if($y -eq 0)
    {

        $names = [array]::CreateInstance([System.String],
$obj.Properties_.Count)
        $values = [array]::CreateInstance([System.String], 4,
$obj.Properties_.Count)
        foreach($prop in $obj.Properties_)
        {
          $names[$x] = $prop.Name
          $values[$y, $x] = GetValue $prop.Name $obj
          $x=$x+1
        }
        $x=0
    }
```

```
    else
    {
      foreach($prop in $obj.Properties_)
      {
        $values[$y, $x] = GetValue $prop.Name $obj
        $x=$x+1
      }
      $x=0
    }
    $y=$y+1
  }
  $ws = New-object -com WScript.Shell
  $fso = New-Object -com Scripting.FileSystemObject
  $txtstream = $fso.OpenTextFile($ws.CurrentDirectory +
"\\Win32_Process.html", 2, $true, -2)
  $txtstream.WriteLine("<html>")
  $txtstream.WriteLine("<head>")
  $txtstream.WriteLine("<title>Win32_Process</title>")
  $txtstream.WriteLine("<style type='text/css'>")
  $txtstream.WriteLine("th")
  $txtstream.WriteLine("{")
  $txtstream.WriteLine("   COLOR: darkred;")
  $txtstream.WriteLine("   BACKGROUND-COLOR: white;")
  $txtstream.WriteLine("   FONT-FAMILY:font-family: Cambria, serif;")
  $txtstream.WriteLine("   FONT-SIZE: 12px;")
  $txtstream.WriteLine("   text-align: left;")
  $txtstream.WriteLine("   white-Space: nowrap;")
  $txtstream.WriteLine("}")
  $txtstream.WriteLine("td")
  $txtstream.WriteLine("{")
  $txtstream.WriteLine("   COLOR: navy;")
  $txtstream.WriteLine("   BACKGROUND-COLOR: white;")
  $txtstream.WriteLine("   FONT-FAMILY: font-family: Cambria, serif;")
```

```
$txtstream.WriteLine("   FONT-SIZE: 12px;")
$txtstream.WriteLine("   text-align: left;")
$txtstream.WriteLine("   white-Space: nowrap;")
$txtstream.WriteLine("}")
$txtstream.WriteLine("</style>")
$txtstream.WriteLine("</head>")
$txtstream.WriteLine("<body>")
#Use this if you want to create a border around your table:
$txtstream.WriteLine("<table Border='0' cellpadding='1' cellspacing='1'>")

#Use this if you don't want to create a border around your table:
$txtstream.WriteLine("<table Border='1' cellpadding='1' cellspacing='1'>")
```

## For Single Line Horizontal

```
$txtstream.WriteLine("<tr>")
for($x=0;$x -lt $names.GetLength(0)-1;$x++)
{
   $txtstream.WriteLine("<th>" + $names[$x] + "</th>")
}
$txtstream.WriteLine("</tr>")
$txtstream.WriteLine("<tr>")
for($x=0;$x -lt $names.GetLength(0)-1;$x++)
{
   [System.String]$value =$values[0, $x]
   $txtstream.WriteLine("<td>" + $value + "</td>")
}
$txtstream.WriteLine("</tr>")
```

## For Multi Line Horizontal

```
$txtstream.WriteLine("<tr>")
for($x=0;$x -lt $names.GetLength(0)-1;$x++)
```

```
    {
        $txtstream.WriteLine("<th>" + $names[$x] + "</th>")
    }
    $txtstream.WriteLine("</tr>")
    for($y=0;$y -lt $values.GetLength(0)-1;$y++)
    {
        $txtstream.WriteLine("<tr>")
        for($x=0;$x -lt $names.GetLength(0)-1;$x++)
        {
            [System.String]$value =$values[$y, $x]
            $txtstream.WriteLine("<td>" + $value + "</td>")
        }
        $txtstream.WriteLine("</tr>")
    }
```

## For Single Line Vertical

```
    $txtstream.WriteLine("<tr>")
    for($x=0;$x -lt $names.GetLength(0)-1;$x++)
    {
        [System.String]$value =$values[0, $x]
        $txtstream.WriteLine("<tr><th>" + $names[$x] + "</th><td>" + $value +
"</td></tr>")
        }
    }
```

## For Multi Line Vertical

```
    $txtstream.WriteLine("<table Border='1' cellpadding='1' cellspacing='1'>")

    for($x=0;$x -lt $names.GetLength(0)-1;$x++)
    {
        $txtstream.WriteLine("<tr><th>" + $names[$x] + "</th>")
```

```
}
for($y=0;$y -lt $values.GetLength(0)-1;$y++)
{
    [System.String]$value =$values[$y, $x]
    $txtstream.WriteLine("<td>" + $value + "</td>")
  }
  $txtstream.WriteLine("</tr>")
}
```

## End Code

```
$txtstream.WriteLine("</table>")
$txtstream.WriteLine("</body>")
$txtstream.WriteLine("</html>")
$txtstream.Close()
```

# Text Delimited File Examples

*Text files can be databases, too*

Below, are code samples for creating various types of delimited files. The getValue function is in Appendix B.

```
function GetValue{

    Param(
    [parameter(position=0)]
    $Name,
    [parameter(position=1)]
    $obj

    )
[string]$PName = $Name + " = "
$tempstr = $obj.GetObjectText_(0)
$pos = $tempstr.IndexOf($PName)
if ($pos -gt 0)
{
    $pos = $pos + $PName.Length
```

```
$tempstr = $tempstr.SubString($pos, ($tempstr.Length - $pos))
$pos = $tempstr.IndexOf(";")
$tempstr = $tempstr.SubString(0, $pos)
$tempstr = $tempstr.Replace('"', "")
$tempstr = $tempstr.Replace("}", "")
$tempstr = $tempstr.Replace("{", "")
$tempstr = $tempstr.Trim()
if($tempstr.Length -gt 14)
{
    if($obj.Properties_.Item($Name).CIMType -eq 101)
    {
        [System.String]$tstr = $tempstr.SubString(4, 2)
        $tstr = $tstr + "/"
        $tstr = $tstr + $tempstr.SubString(6, 2)
        $tstr = $tstr + "/"
        $tstr = $tstr + $tempstr.SubString(0, 4)
        $tstr = $tstr + " "
        $tstr = $tstr + $tempstr.SubString(8, 2)
        $tstr = $tstr + ":"
        $tstr = $tstr + $tempstr.SubString(10, 2)
        $tstr = $tstr + ":"
        $tstr = $tstr + $tempstr.SubString(12, 2)
        $tempstr = $tstr
    }
}
return $tempstr
}
else
{
    return ""
}
}
```

```
[int]$y=0
[int]$x=0
[array]$names = $null
[array]$values = $null
$Locale = "MS_0409"
$Authentication = 6
$Impersonation = 3
$iret = [reflection.assembly]::LoadWithPartialName("'Microsoft.VisualBasic")
$svc = [Microsoft.VisualBasic.Interaction]::GetObject("winmgmts:[locale=" +
$Locale + "]\\.\root\cimv2")
$svc.Security_.AuthenticationLevel = $Authentication
$svc.Security_.ImpersonationLevel= $Impersonation
$strQuery= "Select * From ___InstanceModificationEvent WITHIN 1 where
TargetInstance ISA 'Win32_Process'"
$es = $svc.ExecNotificationQuery($strQuery)
while($y -lt 4)
{
    $ti = $es.NextEvent(-1)
    $obj = $ti.Properties_.Item("TargetInstance").Value
    if($y -eq 0)
    {


        $names = [array]::CreateInstance([System.String],
$obj.Properties_.Count)
        $values = [array]::CreateInstance([System.String], 4,
$obj.Properties_.Count)
        foreach($prop in $obj.Properties_)
        {
          $names[$x] = $prop.Name
          $values[$y, $x] = GetValue $prop.Name $obj
          $x=$x+1
        }
        $x=0
```

```
    }
    else
    {
       foreach($prop in $obj.Properties_)
       {
        $values[$y, $x] = GetValue $prop.Name $obj
        $x=$x+1
       }
       $x=0
    }
    $y=$y+1
}
```

## Colon Delimited

```
$tempstr = ""
$ws = New-object -com WScript.Shell
$fso = New-Object -com Scripting.FileSystemObject
$txtstream = $fso.OpenTextFile($ws.CurrentDirectory +
"\\Win32_Process.txt" , 2, $true, -2)
```

```
for($x=0;$x -lt $names.GetLength(0)-1;$x++)
{
   if($tempstr -ne "")
   {
      $tempstr = $tempstr + ":"
   }
   $tempstr = $tempstr + $name[$x]
}
```

```
$txtstream.WriteLine($tempstr)
$tempstr = ""

for($y=0;$y -lt $values.GetLength(0)-1;$y++)
{
   for($x=0;$x -lt $names.GetLength(0)-1;$x++)
   {
      if($tempstr -ne "")
      {
         $tempstr = $tempstr +  ":";
      }
      [System.String]$value =$values[$y, $x]
      tempstr = $tempstr +  '"' + $value +  '"';
   }
   $txtstream.WriteLine($tempstr)
   $tempstr = ""
}
$txtstream.Close()
```

```
for($x=0;$x -lt $names.GetLength(0)-1;$x++)
{
   $tempstr =  $name{$x]
   for($y=0;$y -lt $values.GetLength(0)-1;$y++)
   {
      if($tempstr -ne "")
      {
         $tempstr = $tempstr +  ":"
      }
      [System.String]$value =$values[$y, $x]
      tempstr = $tempstr +  '"' + $value +  '"'
```

```
    }
    $txtstream.WriteLine($tempstr)
    $tempstr = ""
}
$txtstream.Close()
```

## Comma Delimited

```
$tempstr = ""
$ws = New-object -com WScript.Shell
$fso = New-Object -com Scripting.FileSystemObject
$txtstream = $fso.OpenTextFile($ws.CurrentDirectory +
"\Win32_Process.csv" , 2, $true, -2)
```

HORIZONTAL

```
for($x=0;$x -lt $names.GetLength(0)-1;$x++)
{
    if($tempstr -ne "")
    {
        $tempstr = $tempstr + ","
    }
    $tempstr = $tempstr + $name[$x]
}
$txtstream.WriteLine($tempstr)
$tempstr = ""

for($y=0;$y -lt $values.GetLength(0)-1;$y++)
{
    for($x=0;$x -lt $names.GetLength(0)-1;$x++)
```

```
    {
      if($tempstr -ne "")
      {
        $tempstr = $tempstr +  ":"
      }
      [System.String]$value =$values[$y, $x]
      tempstr = $tempstr +  '"' +  $value +  '"'
    }
    $txtstream.WriteLine($tempstr)
    $tempstr = ""
  }
$txtstream.Close()
```

VERTICAL

```
for($x=0;$x -lt $names.GetLength(0)-1;$x++)
{
  $tempstr =  $name[$x]
  for($y=0;$y -lt $values.GetLength(0)-1;$y++)
  {
    if($tempstr -ne  "")
    {
      $tempstr = $tempstr +  ","
    }
    [System.String]$value =$values[$y, $x]
    tempstr = $tempstr +  '"' +  $value +  '"'
  }
  $txtstream.WriteLine($tempstr)
  $tempstr = ""
}
$txtstream.Close()
```

## Exclamation

```
$tempstr = ""
$ws = New-object -com WScript.Shell
$fso = New-Object -com Scripting.FileSystemObject
$txtstream = $fso.OpenTextFile($ws.CurrentDirectory +
"\\Win32_Process.txt", 2, $true, -2)
```

HORIZONTAL

```
for($x=0;$x -lt $names.GetLength(0)-1;$x++)
{
   if($tempstr -ne "")
   {
      $tempstr = $tempstr +  "!"
   }
   $tempstr = $tempstr +  $name[$x]
}
$txtstream.WriteLine($tempstr)
$tempstr = ""

for($y=0;$y -lt $values.GetLength(0)-1;$y++)
{
   for($x=0;$x -lt $names.GetLength(0)-1;$x++)
   {
      if($tempstr -ne "")
      {
         $tempstr = $tempstr +  "!"
      }
      [System.String]$value =$values[$y, $x]
```

```
        tempstr = $tempstr +  '''' +  $value +  ''''
    }
    $txtstream.WriteLine($tempstr)
    $tempstr = ""
}
$txtstream.Close()
```

---

## VERTICAL

```
for($x=0;$x -lt $names.GetLength(0)-1;$x++)
{
    $tempstr =  $name{$x]
    for($y=0;$y -lt $values.GetLength(0)-1;$y++)
    {
        if($tempstr -ne  "")
        {
            $tempstr = $tempstr +  "!"
        }
        [System.String]$value =$values[$y, $x]
        tempstr = $tempstr +  '''' +  $value +  ''''
    }
    $txtstream.WriteLine($tempstr)
    $tempstr = ""
}
$txtstream.Close()
```

## SEMI COLON

```
$tempstr = ""
$ws = New-object -com WScript.Shell
```

```
$fso = New-Object -com Scripting.FileSystemObject
$txtstream = $fso.OpenTextFile($ws.CurrentDirectory +
"\\Win32_Process.txt", 2, $true, -2)
```

---

```
for($x=0;$x -lt $names.GetLength(0)-1;$x++)
{
   if($tempstr -ne ""“)
   {
      $tempstr = $tempstr +  ";"
   }
   $tempstr = $tempstr +  $name[$x]
}
$txtstream.WriteLine($tempstr)
$tempstr = ""

for($y=0;$y -lt $values.GetLength(0)-1;$y++)
{
   for($x=0;$x -lt $names.GetLength(0)-1;$x++)
   {
      if($tempstr -ne "")
      {
         $tempstr = $tempstr +  ";"
      }
      [System.String]$value =$values[$y, $x]
      tempstr = $tempstr + '"' + $value +  '"'
   }
   $txtstream.WriteLine($tempstr)
   $tempstr = ""
}
$txtstream.Close()
```

78

```
for($x=0;$x -lt $names.GetLength(0)-1;$x++)
{
    $tempstr =  $name[$x]
    for($y=0;$y -lt $values.GetLength(0)-1;$y++)
    {
        if($tempstr -ne "")
        {
            $tempstr = $tempstr +  ";"
        }
        [System.String]$value =$values[$y, $x]
        tempstr = $tempstr +  '"' +  $value +  '"'
    }
    $txtstream.WriteLine($tempstr)
    $tempstr = ""
}
$txtstream.Close()
```

## Tab Delimited

```
$tempstr = ""
$ws = New-object -com WScript.Shell
$fso = New-Object -com Scripting.FileSystemObject
$txtstream = $fso.OpenTextFile($ws.CurrentDirectory +
"\Win32_Process.txt", 2, $true, -2)
```

```
for($x=0;$x -lt $names.GetLength(0)-1;$x++)
{
   if($tempstr -ne "")
   {
      $tempstr = $tempstr +  "\t"
   }
   $tempstr = $tempstr +  $name[$x]
}
$txtstream.WriteLine($tempstr)
$tempstr = ""

for($y=0;$y -lt $values.GetLength(0)-1;$y++)
{
   for($x=0;$x -lt $names.GetLength(0)-1;$x++)
   {
      if($tempstr -ne "")
      {
         $tempstr = $tempstr +  "\t"
      }
      [System.String]$value =$values[$y, $x]
      tempstr = $tempstr + '"' + $value + '"'
   }
   $txtstream.WriteLine($tempstr)
   $tempstr = ""
}
$txtstream.Close()
```

```
for($x=0;$x -lt $names.GetLength(0)-1;$x++)
```

```
    {
      $tempstr =  $name[$x]
      for($y=0;$y -lt $values.GetLength(0)-1;$y++)
      {
        if($tempstr -ne "")
        {
          $tempstr = $tempstr +  "\t"
        }
        [System.String]$value =$values[$y, $x]
        tempstr = $tempstr +  '"' +  $value +  '"'
      }
      $txtstream.WriteLine($tempstr)
      $tempstr = ""
    }
    $txtstream.Close()
```

## Tilde Delimited

```
    $tempstr = "";
    $ws = New-object -com WScript.Shell
    $fso = New-Object -com Scripting.FileSystemObject
    $txtstream = $fso.OpenTextFile($ws.CurrentDirectory +
"\\Win32_Process.txt", 2, $true, -2)
```

```
    for($x=0;$x -lt $names.GetLength(0)-1;$x++)
    {
      if($tempstr -ne "")
```

```
  {
    $tempstr = $tempstr +  "~"
  }
  $tempstr = $tempstr + $name[$x]
}
$txtstream.WriteLine($tempstr)
$tempstr = ""

for($y=0;$y -lt $values.GetLength(0)-1;$y++)
{
  for($x=0;$x -lt $names.GetLength(0)-1;$x++)
  {
    if($tempstr -ne "")
    {
      $tempstr = $tempstr +  "~"
    }
    [System.String]$value =$values[$y, $x]
    tempstr = $tempstr +  '"' + $value +  '"'
  }
  $txtstream.WriteLine($tempstr)
  $tempstr = ""
}
$txtstream.Close()
```

--------------------------------------------------------------------------------

VERTICAL

```
for($x=0;$x -lt $names.GetLength(0)-1;$x++)
{
  $tempstr = $name[$x]
  for($y=0;$y -lt $values.GetLength(0)-1;$y++)
  {
    if($tempstr -ne "")
```

```
        {
            $tempstr = $tempstr +  "~"
        }
        [System.String]$value =$values[$y, $x]
        tempstr = $tempstr + '"' +  $value + '"'
    }
    $txtstream.WriteLine($tempstr)
    $tempstr = ""
}
$txtstream.Close()
```

# THE XML FILES

*Because they are out there*

WELL, I THOUGHT IT WAS CATCHY. Below, are examples of different types of XML that can be used with the MSDAOSP and MSPERSIST Providers. Element XML as a standalone -no XSL referenced – can be used with the MSDAOSP Provider and Schema XML can be used with MSPersist.

```
function GetValue{

    Param(
    [parameter(position=0)]
    $Name,
    [parameter(position=1)]
    $obj
```

```
    )
[string]$PName = $Name + " = "
$tempstr = $obj.GetObjectText_(0)
$pos = $tempstr.IndexOf($PName)
if ($pos -gt 0)
{
    $pos = $pos + $PName.Length
    $tempstr = $tempstr.SubString($pos, ($tempstr.Length - $pos))
    $pos = $tempstr.IndexOf(";")
    $tempstr = $tempstr.SubString(0, $pos)
    $tempstr = $tempstr.Replace('"', "")
    $tempstr = $tempstr.Replace("}", "")
    $tempstr = $tempstr.Replace("{", "")
    $tempstr = $tempstr.Trim()
    if($tempstr.Length -gt 14)
    {
        if($obj.Properties_.Item($Name).CIMType -eq 101)
        {
            [System.String]$tstr = $tempstr.SubString(4, 2)
            $tstr = $tstr + "/"
            $tstr = $tstr + $tempstr.SubString(6, 2)
            $tstr = $tstr + "/"
            $tstr = $tstr + $tempstr.SubString(0, 4)
            $tstr = $tstr + " "
            $tstr = $tstr + $tempstr.SubString(8, 2)
            $tstr = $tstr + ":"
            $tstr = $tstr + $tempstr.SubString(10, 2)
            $tstr = $tstr + ":"
            $tstr = $tstr + $tempstr.SubString(12, 2)
            $tempstr = $tstr
        }
    }
    return $tempstr
```

```
        }
        else
        {
            return ""
        }
    }

    [int]$y=0
    [int]$x=0
    [array]$names = $null
    [array]$values = $null
    $Locale = "MS_0409"
    $Authentication = 6
    $Impersonation = 3
    $iret = [reflection.assembly]::LoadWithPartialName("'Microsoft.VisualBasic")
    $svc = [Microsoft.VisualBasic.Interaction]::GetObject("winmgmts:[locale=" +
$Locale + "]\\.\root\cimv2")
    $svc.Security_.AuthenticationLevel = $Authentication
    $svc.Security_.ImpersonationLevel= $Impersonation
    $strQuery= "Select * From ___InstanceModificationEvent WITHIN 1 where
TargetInstance ISA 'Win32_Process'"
    $es = $svc.ExecNotificationQuery($strQuery)
    while($y -lt 4)
    {
        $ti = $es.NextEvent(-1)
        $obj = $ti.Properties_.Item("TargetInstance").Value
        if($y -eq 0)
        {

            $names = [array]::CreateInstance([System.String],
$obj.Properties_.Count)
            $values = [array]::CreateInstance([System.String], 4,
$obj.Properties_.Count)
```

```
      foreach($prop in $obj.Properties_)
      {
       $names[$x] = $prop.Name
       $values[$y, $x] = GetValue $prop.Name $obj
       $x=$x+1
      }
      $x=0
    }
    else
    {
      foreach($prop in $obj.Properties_)
      {
       $values[$y, $x] = GetValue $prop.Name $obj
       $x=$x+1
      }
      $x=0
    }
    $y=$y+1
  }
```

## Element XML

```
  $ws = New-object -com WScript.Shell
  $fso = New-Object -com Scripting.FileSystemObject
  $txtstream = $fso.OpenTextFile($ws.CurrentDirectory +
"\\Win32_Process.xml", 2, $true, -2)
  $txtstream.WriteLine("<?xml version='1.0' encoding='iso-8859-1'?>")
  $txtstream.WriteLine("<data>")
  for($y=0;$y -lt $values.GetLength(0)-1;$y++)
  {
    $txtstream.WriteLine("<Win32_process>")
    for($x=0;$x -lt $names.GetLength(0)-1;$x++)
    {
```

```
          [System.String]$value =$values[$y, $x]
          $txtstream.WriteLine("<" + $names[$x] + ">" + $value + "</" +
$names[$x] + ">")
     }
     $txtstream.WriteLine("</Win32_process>")
  }
  $txtstream.WriteLine("</data>")
  $txtstream.Close()
```

WMI to Element XML For XSL

```
  $ws = New-object -com WScript.Shell
  $fso = New-Object -com Scripting.FileSystemObject
  $txtstream = $fso.OpenTextFile($ws.CurrentDirectory +
"\\Win32_Process.xml", 2, $true, -2)
  $txtstream.WriteLine("<?xml version='1.0' encoding='iso-8859-1'?>")
  $txtstream.WriteLine("<?xml-stylesheet type='Text/xsl' href=""" +
ws.CurrentDirectory +  "\\Win32_Process.xsl""?>")

  for($y=0;$y -lt $values.GetLength(0)-1;$y++)
  {
     $txtstream.WriteLine("<Win32_process>")
     for($x=0;$x -lt $names.GetLength(0)-1;$x++)
     {
          [System.String]$value =$values[$y, $x]
          $txtstream.WriteLine("<" + $names[$x] + ">" + $value + "</" +
$names[$x] + ">")
     }
     $txtstream.WriteLine("</Win32_process>")
  }
  $txtstream.WriteLine("</data>")
  $txtstream.Close()
```

## SCHEMA XML

```
$ws = New-object -com WScript.Shell
$fso = New-Object -com Scripting.FileSystemObject
$txtstream = $fso.OpenTextFile($ws.CurrentDirectory +
"\\Win32_Process.xml", 2, $true, -2)
$txtstream.WriteLine("<?xml version='1.0' encoding='iso-8859-1'?>")
$txtstream.WriteLine("<data>")
for($y=0;$y -lt $values.GetLength(0)-1;$y++)
{
    $txtstream.WriteLine("<Win32_process>")
    for($x=0;$x -lt $names.GetLength(0)-1;$x++)
    {
        [System.String]$value =$values[$y, $x]
        $txtstream.WriteLine("<" + $names[$x] + ">" + $value + "</" +
$names[$x] + ">")
    }
    $txtstream.WriteLine("</Win32_process>")
}
$txtstream.WriteLine("</data>")
$txtstream.Close()

$rs1 = New-object -com ADODB.Recordset
$rs1.ActiveConnection = "Provider=MSDAOSP; Data
Source=msxml2.DSOControl"
$rs1.Open(ws.CurrentDirectory + "\\Win32_Process.xml")

if($fso.FileExists(ws.CurrentDirectory + "\\Win32_Process_Schema.xml") eq
$true)
{
    $fso.DeleteFile($ws.CurrentDirectory + "\\Win32_Process_Schema.xml")
```

```
}
$rs1..Save($ws.CurrentDirectory +  "\\Win32_Process_Schema.xml, 1) ;
```

# EXCEL
## Three ways to get the job done

THERE ARE THREE WAYS TO PUT DATA INTO EXCEL. CREATE A COMA DELIMITED FILE AND THEN USE WS.RUN, THROUGH AUTOMATION AND BY CREATING A PHYSICAL SPREADSHEET. Below are examples of doing exactly that.

```
function GetValue{

    Param(
    [parameter(position=0)]
    $Name,
    [parameter(position=1)]
    $obj
    )

    [string]$PName = $Name + " = "
    $tempstr = $obj.GetObjectText_(0)
    $pos = $tempstr.IndexOf($PName)
    if ($pos -gt 0)
    {
```

```
$pos = $pos + $PName.Length
$tempstr = $tempstr.SubString($pos, ($tempstr.Length - $pos))
$pos = $tempstr.IndexOf(";")
$tempstr = $tempstr.SubString(0, $pos)
$tempstr = $tempstr.Replace('"', "")
$tempstr = $tempstr.Replace("}", "")
$tempstr = $tempstr.Replace("{", "")
$tempstr = $tempstr.Trim()
if($tempstr.Length -gt 14)
{
    if($obj.Properties_.Item($Name).CIMType -eq 101)
    {
        [System.String]$tstr = $tempstr.SubString(4, 2)
        $tstr = $tstr + "/"
        $tstr = $tstr + $tempstr.SubString(6, 2)
        $tstr = $tstr + "/"
        $tstr = $tstr + $tempstr.SubString(0, 4)
        $tstr = $tstr + " "
        $tstr = $tstr + $tempstr.SubString(8, 2)
        $tstr = $tstr + ":"
        $tstr = $tstr + $tempstr.SubString(10, 2)
        $tstr = $tstr + ":"
        $tstr = $tstr + $tempstr.SubString(12, 2)
        $tempstr = $tstr
    }
}
return $tempstr
}
else
{
    return ""
}
}
```

```
[int]$y=0
[int]$x=0
[array]$names = $null
[array]$values = $null
$Locale = "MS_0409"
$Authentication = 6
$Impersonation = 3
$iret = [reflection.assembly]::LoadWithPartialName("'Microsoft.VisualBasic")
$svc = [Microsoft.VisualBasic.Interaction]::GetObject("winmgmts:[locale=" +
$Locale + "]\\.\root\cimv2")
$svc.Security_.AuthenticationLevel = $Authentication
$svc.Security_.ImpersonationLevel= $Impersonation
$strQuery= "Select * From ___InstanceModificationEvent WITHIN 1 where
TargetInstance ISA 'Win32_Process'"
$es = $svc.ExecNotificationQuery($strQuery)
while($y -lt 4)
{
   $ti = $es.NextEvent(-1)
   $obj = $ti.Properties_.Item("TargetInstance").Value
   if($y -eq 0)
   {

       $names = [array]::CreateInstance([System.String],
$obj.Properties_.Count)
       $values = [array]::CreateInstance([System.String], 4,
$obj.Properties_.Count)
      foreach($prop in $obj.Properties_)
      {
        $names[$x] = $prop.Name
        $values[$y, $x] = GetValue $prop.Name $obj
        $x=$x+1
      }
```

```
        $x=0
    }
    else
    {
        foreach($prop in $obj.Properties_)
        {
            $values[$y, $x] = GetValue $prop.Name $obj
            $x=$x+1
        }
        $x=0
    }
    $y=$y+1
}
```

## Using the comma delimited file

```
$tempstr = "";
$ws = New-object -com WScript.Shell
$fso = New-object -com  ("Scripting.FileSystemObject
$txtstream = $fso.OpenTextFile($ws.CurrentDirectory +
"\\Win32_Process.csv" , 2, $true, -2)
```

---

HORIZONTAL

```
for($x=0;$x -lt $names.GetLength(0)-1;$x++)
{
    if($tempstr -ne "")
    {
        $tempstr = $tempstr +  ","
    }
    $tempstr = $tempstr +  $name[$x]
```

```
}
$txtstream.WriteLine($tempstr)
$tempstr = ""

for($y=0;$y -lt $values.GetLength(0)-1;$y++)
{
   for($x=0;$x -lt $names.GetLength(0)-1;$x++)
   {
      if($tempstr -ne "")
      {
         $tempstr = $tempstr + ":"
      }
      [System.String]$value =$values[$y, $x]
      tempstr = $tempstr + '"' + $value + '"'
   }
   $txtstream.WriteLine($tempstr)
   $tempstr = ""
}
$txtstream.Close()
```

---

VERTICAL

```
for($x=0;$x -lt $names.GetLength(0)-1;$x++)
{
   $tempstr = $name[$x]
   for($y=0;$y -lt $values.GetLength(0)-1;$y++)
   {
      if($tempstr -ne "")
      {
         $tempstr = $tempstr + ","
      }
      [System.String]$value =$values[$y, $x]
```

```
      tempstr = $tempstr + '"' + $value + '"'
    }
    $txtstream.WriteLine($tempstr)
    $tempstr = ""
}
$txtstream.Close()
$ws.Run($ws.CurrentDirectory +  "\\Win32_Process.csv")
```

Excel Automation

---

HORIZONTAL VIEW

```
$oExcel = New-object -com Excel.Application
$oExcel.Visible = $true;
$wb = $oExcel.Workbooks.Add()
$ws = $wb.Worksheets
$ws.Name = "Win32_Process";
for($x=0;$x -lt $names.GetLength(0)-1;$x++)
{
    $ws.Cells.Item(1, $x+1) = $prop.Name;
    $x=$x. 1;
}
$x=1;
for($y=0;$y -lt $values.GetLength(0)-1;$y++)
{
    for($x=0;$x -lt $names.GetLength(0)-1;$x++)
    {
      [System.String]$value =$values[$y, $x]
      $ws.Cells.Item($y+1, $x+1) = $values[$y, $x]
```

```
        }
    }
    $ws.Columns.HorizontalAlignment = -4131;
    $ws.Columns.AutoFit()
```

---

## FOR A VERTICAL VIEW

```
$oExcel = New-object -com Excel.Application
$oExcel.Visible = $true;
$wb = $oExcel.Workbooks.Add()
$ws = $wb.Worksheets
$ws.Name = "Win32_Process";
for($x=0;$x -lt $names.GetLength(0)-1;$x++)
{
    $ws.Cells.Item($x+1, 1) = $prop.Name;
    $x=$x. 1;
}
$x=1;
for($y=0;$y -lt $values.GetLength(0)-1;$y++)
{
    for($x=0;$x -lt $names.GetLength(0)-1;$x++)
    {
        [System.String]$value =$values[$y, $x]
        $ws.Cells.Item($x+1, $y+1) = $values[$y, $x]
    }
}
$ws.Columns.HorizontalAlignment = -4131;
$ws.Columns.AutoFit()
```

## Using A Spreadsheet

```
$ws = New-object -com WScript.Shell
$fso = New-object -com Scripting.FileSystemObject
$txtstream = $fso.OpenTextFile($ws.CurrentDirectory + "\\ProcessExcel.xml",
2, $true, -2)
$txtstream.WriteLine("<?xml version='1.0'?>")
$txtstream.WriteLine("<?mso-application progid='Excel.Sheet'?>")
$txtstream.WriteLine("<Workbook xmlns='urn:schemas-microsoft-
com:office:spreadsheet' xmlns:o='urn:schemas-microsoft-com:office:office'
xmlns:x='urn:schemas-microsoft-com:office:excel' xmlns:ss='urn:schemas-
microsoft-com:office:spreadsheet' xmlns:html='http://www.w3.org/TR/REC-
html40'>")
$txtstream.WriteLine("        <Document$properties xmlns='urn:schemas-
microsoft-com:office:office'>")
$txtstream.WriteLine("                    <Author>Windows User</Author>")
$txtstream.WriteLine("                    <LastAuthor>Windows
User</LastAuthor>")
$txtstream.WriteLine("                    <Created>2007-11-
27T19:36:16Z</Created>")
$txtstream.WriteLine("                    <Version>12.00</Version>")
$txtstream.WriteLine("        </Document$properties>")
$txtstream.WriteLine("        <ExcelWorkbook xmlns='urn:schemas-
microsoft-com:office:excel'>")
$txtstream.WriteLine("
    <WindowHeight>11835</WindowHeight>")
$txtstream.WriteLine("
    <WindowWidth>18960</WindowWidth>")
$txtstream.WriteLine("                    <WindowTopX>120</WindowTopX>")
$txtstream.WriteLine("                    <WindowTopY>135</WindowTopY>")
$txtstream.WriteLine("
    <ProtectStructure>False</ProtectStructure>")
$txtstream.WriteLine("
    <ProtectWindows>False</ProtectWindows>")
```

```
$txtstream.WriteLine("        </ExcelWorkbook>")
$txtstream.WriteLine("        <Styles>")
$txtstream.WriteLine("            <Style ss:ID='Default'
ss:Name='Normal'>")
$txtstream.WriteLine("                <Alignment
ss:Vertical='Bottom'/>")
$txtstream.WriteLine("                <Borders/>")
$txtstream.WriteLine("                <Font ss:FontName='Calibri'
x:Family='Swiss' ss:Size='11' ss:Color='#000000'/>")
$txtstream.WriteLine("                <Interior/>")
$txtstream.WriteLine("                <NumberFormat/>")
$txtstream.WriteLine("                <Protection/>")
$txtstream.WriteLine("            </Style>")
$txtstream.WriteLine("            <Style ss:ID='s62'>")
$txtstream.WriteLine("                <Borders/>")
$txtstream.WriteLine("                <Font ss:FontName='Calibri'
x:Family='Swiss' ss:Size='11' ss:Color='#000000' ss:Bold='1'/>")
$txtstream.WriteLine("            </Style>")
$txtstream.WriteLine("            <Style ss:ID='s63'>")
$txtstream.WriteLine("                <Alignment
ss:Horizontal='Left' ss:Vertical='Bottom' ss:Indent='2'/>")
$txtstream.WriteLine("                <Font ss:FontName='Verdana'
x:Family='Swiss' ss:Size='7.7' ss:Color='#000000'/>")
$txtstream.WriteLine("            </Style>")
$txtstream.WriteLine("    </Styles>")
$txtstream.WriteLine("<Worksheet ss:Name='Process'>")
$txtstream.WriteLine("    <Table x:FullColumns='1' x:FullRows='1'
ss:DefaultRowHeight='24.9375'>")
$txtstream.WriteLine("        <Column ss:AutoFitWidth='1' ss:Width='82.5'
ss:Span='5'/>")
$txtstream.WriteLine("        <Row ss:AutoFitHeight='0'>")
for($x=0;$x -lt $names.GetLength(0)-1;$x++)
{
```

```
        $txtstream.WriteLine("        <Cell ss:StyleID='s62'><Data
ss:Type='String'>" + $names[$x] + "</Data></Cell>")
    }
    $txtstream.WriteLine("      </Row>")


    for($y=0;$y -lt $values.GetLength(0)-1;$y++)
    {
      $txtstream.WriteLine("      <Row ss:AutoFitHeight='0' ss:Height='13.5'>")
      for($x=0;$x -lt $names.GetLength(0)-1;$x++)
      {
        [System.String]$value =$values[$y, $x]
        $txtstream.WriteLine("        <Cell><Data ss:Type='String'><![CDATA[" +
$value + "]]></Data></Cell>")
      }
      $txtstream.WriteLine("      </Row>")
    }
    $txtstream.WriteLine("  </Table>")
    $txtstream.WriteLine("        <WorksheetOptions xmlns='urn:schemas-
microsoft-com:office:excel'>")
    $txtstream.WriteLine("              <PageSetup>")
    $txtstream.WriteLine("                  <Header x:Margin='0.3'/>")
    $txtstream.WriteLine("                  <Footer x:Margin='0.3'/>")
    $txtstream.WriteLine("                  <PageMargins x:Bottom='0.75'
x:Left='0.7' x:Right='0.7' x:Top='0.75'/>")
    $txtstream.WriteLine("              </PageSetup>")
    $txtstream.WriteLine("          <Unsynced/>")
    $txtstream.WriteLine("          <Print>")
    $txtstream.WriteLine("                  <FitHeight>0</FitHeight>")
    $txtstream.WriteLine("                  <ValidPrinterInfo/>")
    $txtstream.WriteLine("
        <HorizontalResolution>600</HorizontalResolution>")
```

```
$txtstream.WriteLine("
    <VerticalResolution>600</VerticalResolution>")
$txtstream.WriteLine("                    </Print>")
$txtstream.WriteLine("                    <Selected/>")
$txtstream.WriteLine("                    <Panes>")
$txtstream.WriteLine("                        <Pane>")
$txtstream.WriteLine("
    <Number>3</Number>")
$txtstream.WriteLine("
    <ActiveRow>9</ActiveRow>")
$txtstream.WriteLine("
    <ActiveCol>7</ActiveCol>")
$txtstream.WriteLine("                        </Pane>")
$txtstream.WriteLine("                    </Panes>")
$txtstream.WriteLine("
    <ProtectObjects>False</ProtectObjects>")
$txtstream.WriteLine("
    <ProtectScenarios>False</ProtectScenarios>")
$txtstream.WriteLine("        </WorksheetOptions>")
$txtstream.WriteLine("</Worksheet>")
$txtstream.WriteLine("</Workbook>")
$txtstream.Close()()
ws.Run(ws.CurrentDirectory + "\ProcessExcel.xml")
```

# XSL
## The end of the line

BELOW ARE WAYS YOU CAN CREATE XSL FILES TO RENDER YOU XML. Viewer discretion is advised.

```
function GetValue{

    Param(
    [parameter(position=0)]
    $Name,
    [parameter(position=1)]
    $obj

    )
    [string]$PName = $Name + " = "
    $tempstr = $obj.GetObjectText_(0)
    $pos = $tempstr.IndexOf($PName)
    if ($pos -gt 0)
    {
        $pos = $pos + $PName.Length
        $tempstr = $tempstr.SubString($pos, ($tempstr.Length - $pos))
```

```
$pos = $tempstr.IndexOf(";")
$tempstr = $tempstr.SubString(0, $pos)
$tempstr = $tempstr.Replace("'", "")
$tempstr = $tempstr.Replace("}", "")
$tempstr = $tempstr.Replace("{", "")
$tempstr = $tempstr.Trim()
if($tempstr.Length -gt 14)
{
    if($obj.Properties_.Item($Name).CIMType -eq 101)
    {
        [System.String]$tstr = $tempstr.SubString(4, 2)
        $tstr = $tstr + "/"
        $tstr = $tstr + $tempstr.SubString(6, 2)
        $tstr = $tstr + "/"
        $tstr = $tstr + $tempstr.SubString(0, 4)
        $tstr = $tstr + " "
        $tstr = $tstr + $tempstr.SubString(8, 2)
        $tstr = $tstr + ":"
        $tstr = $tstr + $tempstr.SubString(10, 2)
        $tstr = $tstr + ":"
        $tstr = $tstr + $tempstr.SubString(12, 2)
        $tempstr = $tstr
    }
}
    return $tempstr
}
else
{
    return ""
}
}


[int]$y=0
```

```
[int]$x=0
[array]$names = $null
[array]$values = $null
$Locale = "MS_0409"
$Authentication = 6
$Impersonation = 3
$iret = [reflection.assembly]::LoadWithPartialName("'Microsoft.VisualBasic")
$svc = [Microsoft.VisualBasic.Interaction]::GetObject("winmgmts:[locale=" +
$Locale + "]\\.\root\cimv2")
$svc.Security_.AuthenticationLevel = $Authentication
$svc.Security_.ImpersonationLevel= $Impersonation
$strQuery= "Select * From ___InstanceModificationEvent WITHIN 1 where
TargetInstance ISA 'Win32_Process'"
$es = $svc.ExecNotificationQuery($strQuery)
while($y -lt 4)
{
    $ti = $es.NextEvent(-1)
    $obj = $ti.Properties_.Item("TargetInstance").Value
    if($y -eq 0)
    {

        $names = [array]::CreateInstance([System.String],
$obj.Properties_.Count)
        $values = [array]::CreateInstance([System.String], 4,
$obj.Properties_.Count)
        foreach($prop in $obj.Properties_)
        {
          $names[$x] = $prop.Name
          $values[$y, $x] = GetValue $prop.Name $obj
          $x=$x+1
        }
        $x=0
    }
```

```
    else
    {
      foreach($prop in $obj.Properties_)
      {
        $values[$y, $x] = GetValue $prop.Name $obj
        $x=$x+1
      }
      $x=0
    }
    $y=$y+1
  }
```

```
$ws = New-object -com WScript.Shell
$fso = New-object -com Scripting.FileSystemObject
$txtstream= $fso.OpenTextFile($ws.CurrentDirectory +  "\\Process.xsl", 2,
$true, -2)
```

## SINGLE LINE HORIZONTAL

```
$txtstream.WriteLine("<?xml version=""1.0" " encoding=""UTF-8" "?>")
$txtstream.WriteLine("<xsl:stylesheet version=""1.0""
xmlns:xsl=""http://www.w3.org/1999/XSL/Transform" ">")
$txtstream.WriteLine("<xsl:template match=""/""">")
$txtstream.WriteLine("<html>")
$txtstream.WriteLine("<head>")
```

```
$txtstream.WriteLine("<title>Products</title>")
$txtstream.WriteLine("<style type='text/css'>")
$txtstream.WriteLine("th")
$txtstream.WriteLine("{")
$txtstream.WriteLine("    COLOR: darkred;")
$txtstream.WriteLine("    BACKGROUND-COLOR: white;")
$txtstream.WriteLine("    FONT-FAMILY:font-family: Cambria, serif;")
$txtstream.WriteLine("    FONT-SIZE: 12px;")
$txtstream.WriteLine("    text-align: left;")
$txtstream.WriteLine("    white-Space: nowrap;")
$txtstream.WriteLine("}")
$txtstream.WriteLine("td")
$txtstream.WriteLine("{")
$txtstream.WriteLine("    COLOR: navy;")
$txtstream.WriteLine("    BACKGROUND-COLOR: white;")
$txtstream.WriteLine("    FONT-FAMILY: font-family: Cambria, serif;")
$txtstream.WriteLine("    FONT-SIZE: 12px;")
$txtstream.WriteLine("    text-align: left;")
$txtstream.WriteLine("    white-Space: nowrap;")
$txtstream.WriteLine("}")
$txtstream.WriteLine("</style>")
$txtstream.WriteLine("</head>")
$txtstream.WriteLine("<body bgcolor=""#333333"">")
$txtstream.WriteLine("<table colspacing=""3"" colpadding=""3"">")
$txtstream.WriteLine("<tr>")
for($x=0;$x -lt $names.GetLength(0)-1;$x++)
{
    $txtstream.WriteLine("<th>" + $names[$x] + </th>")
}
$txtstream.WriteLine("</tr>")
$txtstream.WriteLine("<tr>")
for($x=0;$x -lt $names.GetLength(0)-1;$x++)
{
```

```
$txtstream.WriteLine("<td><xsl:value-of select=""data/Win32_Process/" +
$names[$x] + """/></td>")
    }
$txtstream.WriteLine("</tr>")
$txtstream.WriteLine("</table>")
$txtstream.WriteLine("</body>")
$txtstream.WriteLine("</html>")
$txtstream.WriteLine("</xsl:template>")
$txtstream.WriteLine("</xsl:stylesheet>")
$txtstream.Close()()
```

## For Multi Line Horizontal

```
$txtstream.WriteLine("<?xml version=""1.0" " encoding=""UTF-8" "?>")
$txtstream.WriteLine("<xsl:stylesheet version=""1.0""
xmlns:xsl=""http://www.w3.org/1999/XSL/Transform" ">")
$txtstream.WriteLine("<xsl:template match=""/""">")
$txtstream.WriteLine("<html>")
$txtstream.WriteLine("<head>")
$txtstream.WriteLine("<title>Products</title>")
$txtstream.WriteLine("<style type='text/css'>")
$txtstream.WriteLine("th")
$txtstream.WriteLine("{")
$txtstream.WriteLine("    COLOR: darkred;")
$txtstream.WriteLine("    BACKGROUND-COLOR: white;")
$txtstream.WriteLine("    FONT-FAMILY:font-family: Cambria, serif;")
$txtstream.WriteLine("    FONT-SIZE: 12px;")
$txtstream.WriteLine("    text-align: left;")
$txtstream.WriteLine("    white-Space: nowrap;")
$txtstream.WriteLine("}")
$txtstream.WriteLine("td")
```

```
$txtstream.WriteLine("{")
$txtstream.WriteLine("    COLOR: navy;")
$txtstream.WriteLine("    BACKGROUND-COLOR: white;")
$txtstream.WriteLine("    FONT-FAMILY: font-family: Cambria, serif;")
$txtstream.WriteLine("    FONT-SIZE: 12px;")
$txtstream.WriteLine("    text-align: left;")
$txtstream.WriteLine("    white-Space: nowrap;")
$txtstream.WriteLine("}")
$txtstream.WriteLine("</style>")
$txtstream.WriteLine("</head>")
$txtstream.WriteLine("<body bgcolor=""#333333" ">")
$txtstream.WriteLine("<table colspacing=""3" " colpadding=""3" ">")
$txtstream.WriteLine("<tr>")
for($x=0;$x -lt $names.GetLength(0)-1;$x++)
{
    $txtstream.WriteLine("<th>" + $names[$x] + </th>")
}
$txtstream.WriteLine("</tr>")
$txtstream.WriteLine("<xsl:for-each select=""data/Win32_Process"">")
$txtstream.WriteLine("<tr>")
for($x=0;$x -lt $names.GetLength(0)-1;$x++)
{
    $txtstream.WriteLine("<td><xsl:value-of select="" + $names[$x] +
"""/></td>")
}
$txtstream.WriteLine("</tr>")
$txtstream.WriteLine("</xsl:for-each>")
$txtstream.WriteLine("</table>")
$txtstream.WriteLine("</body>")
$txtstream.WriteLine("</html>")
$txtstream.WriteLine("</xsl:template>")
$txtstream.WriteLine("</xsl:stylesheet>")
$txtstream.Close()()
```

## For Single Line Vertical

```
$txtstream.WriteLine("<?xml version=""1.0" " encoding=""UTF-8" "?>")
$txtstream.WriteLine("<xsl:stylesheet version=""1.0""
xmlns:xsl=""http://www.w3.org/1999/XSL/Transform" ">")
$txtstream.WriteLine("<xsl:template match=""/""">")
$txtstream.WriteLine("<html>")
$txtstream.WriteLine("<head>")
$txtstream.WriteLine("<title>Products</title>")
$txtstream.WriteLine("<style type='text/css'>")
$txtstream.WriteLine("th")
$txtstream.WriteLine("{")
$txtstream.WriteLine("    COLOR: darkred;")
$txtstream.WriteLine("    BACKGROUND-COLOR: white;")
$txtstream.WriteLine("    FONT-FAMILY:font-family: Cambria, serif;")
$txtstream.WriteLine("    FONT-SIZE: 12px;")
$txtstream.WriteLine("    text-align: left;")
$txtstream.WriteLine("    white-Space: nowrap;")
$txtstream.WriteLine("}")
$txtstream.WriteLine("td")
$txtstream.WriteLine("{")
$txtstream.WriteLine("    COLOR: navy;")
$txtstream.WriteLine("    BACKGROUND-COLOR: white;")
$txtstream.WriteLine("    FONT-FAMILY: font-family: Cambria, serif;")
$txtstream.WriteLine("    FONT-SIZE: 12px;")
$txtstream.WriteLine("    text-align: left;")
$txtstream.WriteLine("    white-Space: nowrap;")
$txtstream.WriteLine("}")
$txtstream.WriteLine("</style>")
$txtstream.WriteLine("</head>")
$txtstream.WriteLine("<body bgcolor=""#333333" ">")
```

```
$txtstream.WriteLine("<table colspacing=""3" " colpadding=""3" ">")

for($x=0;$x -lt $names.GetLength(0)-1;$x++)
{
    $txtstream.WriteLine("<tr><th>" + $names[$x] + </th>")
    $txtstream.WriteLine("<td><xsl:value-of select="""data/Win32_Process/" +
$names[$x] + """/></td></tr>")
}
$txtstream.WriteLine("</table>")
$txtstream.WriteLine("</body>")
$txtstream.WriteLine("</html>")
$txtstream.WriteLine("</xsl:template>")
$txtstream.WriteLine("</xsl:stylesheet>")
$txtstream.Close()
```

## For Multi Line Vertical

```
$txtstream.WriteLine("<?xml version=""1.0" " encoding=""UTF-8" "?>")
$txtstream.WriteLine("<xsl:stylesheet version=""1.0""
xmlns:xsl=""http://www.w3.org/1999/XSL/Transform" ">")
$txtstream.WriteLine("<xsl:template match=""/""">")
$txtstream.WriteLine("<html>")
$txtstream.WriteLine("<head>")
$txtstream.WriteLine("<title>Products</title>")
$txtstream.WriteLine("<style type='text/css'>")
$txtstream.WriteLine("th")
$txtstream.WriteLine("{")
$txtstream.WriteLine("   COLOR: darkred;")
$txtstream.WriteLine("   BACKGROUND-COLOR: white;")
$txtstream.WriteLine("   FONT-FAMILY:font-family: Cambria, serif;")
$txtstream.WriteLine("   FONT-SIZE: 12px;")
$txtstream.WriteLine("   text-align: left;")
$txtstream.WriteLine("   white-Space: nowrap;")
```

```
$txtstream.WriteLine("}")
$txtstream.WriteLine("td")
$txtstream.WriteLine("{")
$txtstream.WriteLine("   COLOR: navy;")
$txtstream.WriteLine("   BACKGROUND-COLOR: white;")
$txtstream.WriteLine("   FONT-FAMILY: font-family: Cambria, serif;")
$txtstream.WriteLine("   FONT-SIZE: 12px;")
$txtstream.WriteLine("   text-align: left;")
$txtstream.WriteLine("   white-Space: nowrap;")
$txtstream.WriteLine("}")
$txtstream.WriteLine("</style>")
$txtstream.WriteLine("</head>")
$txtstream.WriteLine("<body bgcolor=""#333333" ">")
$txtstream.WriteLine("<table colspacing=""3" " colpadding=""3" ">")

$txtstream.WriteLine("<tr>")
for($x=0;$x -lt $names.GetLength(0)-1;$x++)
{
    $txtstream.WriteLine("<tr><th>" + $names[$x] + </th>")
    $txtstream.WriteLine("<td><xsl:for-each
select=""data/Win32_Process"">")
    $txtstream.WriteLine("<xsl:value-of select=""" + $names[$x] +
"""/></td>")
    $txtstream.WriteLine("</xsl:for-each></tr>")
next
$txtstream.WriteLine("</table>")
$txtstream.WriteLine("</body>")
$txtstream.WriteLine("</html>")
$txtstream.WriteLine("</xsl:template>")
$txtstream.WriteLine("</xsl:stylesheet>")
$txtstream.Close()
```

# Stylesheets

*The difference between boring and oh, wow!*

THE FIRST PARAGRAPH STYLE GIVES you nice spacing after the title, as well as the right indents for the first part of your text. Try adding uppercase letters to half of the first line for added styling.  For even more stylistic impact, add a

Style sheets:

The stylesheets in Appendix A, were used to render these pages. If you find one you like, feel free to use it.

Report:

Table

| ProductID | ProductName | SupplierID | CategoryID | QuantityPerUnit | UnitPrice | UnitsInStock | UnitsOnOrder | ReorderLevel | Discontinued |
|-----------|-------------|------------|------------|-----------------|-----------|--------------|--------------|--------------|--------------|
| 1 | Chai | 1 | 1 | 10 boxes x 20 bags | 18 | 39 | 0 | 10 | False |
| 2 | Chang | 1 | 1 | 24 - 12 oz bottles | 19 | 17 | 40 | 25 | False |
| 3 | Aniseed Syrup | 1 | 2 | 12 - 550 ml bottles | 10 | 13 | 70 | 25 | False |
| 4 | Chef Anton's Cajun Seasoning | 2 | 2 | 48 - 6 oz jars | 22 | 53 | 0 | 0 | False |
| 5 | Chef Anton's Gumbo Mix | 2 | 2 | 36 boxes | 21.35 | 0 | 0 | 0 | True |
| 6 | Grandma's Boysenberry Spread | 3 | 2 | 12 - 8 oz jars | 25 | 120 | 0 | 25 | False |
| 7 | Uncle Bob's Organic Dried Pears | 3 | 7 | 12 - 1 lb pkgs. | 30 | 15 | 0 | 10 | False |
| 8 | Northwoods Cranberry Sauce | 3 | 2 | 12 - 12 oz jars | 40 | 6 | 0 | 0 | False |
| 9 | Mishi Kobe Niku | 4 | 6 | 18 - 500 g pkgs. | 97 | 29 | 0 | 0 | True |
| 10 | Ikura | 4 | 8 | 12 - 200 ml jars | 31 | 31 | 0 | 0 | False |
| 11 | Queso Cabrales | 5 | 4 | 1 kg pkg. | 21 | 22 | 30 | 30 | False |
| 12 | Queso Manchego La Pastora | 5 | 4 | 10 - 500 g pkgs. | 38 | 86 | 0 | 0 | False |
| 13 | Konbu | 6 | 8 | 2 kg box | 6 | 24 | 0 | 5 | False |
| 14 | Tofu | 6 | 7 | 40 - 100 g pkgs. | 23.25 | 35 | 0 | 0 | False |
| 15 | Genen Shouyu | 6 | 2 | 24 - 250 ml bottles | 15.5 | 39 | 0 | 5 | False |

None:

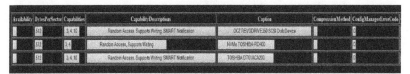

Black and White

Colored:

115

| AccountExpires | AuthorizationFlags | BadPasswordCount | Caption | CodePage | Comment | CountryCode | Description |
|---|---|---|---|---|---|---|---|
| | | | NT AUTHORITY\SYSTEM | | | | Network login profile settings for SYSTEM on NT AUTHORITY |
| | | | NT AUTHORITY\LOCAL SERVICE | | | | Network login profile settings for LOCAL SERVICE on NT AUTHORITY |
| | | | NT AUTHORITY\NETWORK SERVICE | | | | Network login profile settings for NETWORK SERVICE on NT AUTHORITY |
| | 0 | 0 | Administrator | 0 | Built-in account for administering the computer/domain | 0 | Network login profile settings for on WIN-SWLOAKMF7JB |
| | | | NT SERVICE\SSASTELEMETRY | | | | Network login profile settings for SSASTELEMETRY on NT SERVICE |
| | | | NT SERVICE\SSISTELEMETRY130 | | | | Network login profile settings for SSISTELEMETRY130 on NT SERVICE |
| | | | NT SERVICE\SQLTELEMETRY | | | | Network login profile settings for SQLTELEMETRY on NT SERVICE |
| | | | NT SERVICE\MSSQLServerOLAPService | | | | Network login profile settings for MSSQLServerOLAPService on NT SERVICE |
| | | | NT SERVICE\ReportServer | | | | Network login profile settings for ReportServer on NT SERVICE |
| | | | NT SERVICE\MSSQLFDLauncher | | | | Network login profile settings for MSSQLFDLauncher on NT SERVICE |
| | | | NT SERVICE\MSSQLLaunchpad | | | | Network login profile settings for MSSQLLaunchpad on NT SERVICE |
| | | | NT SERVICE\MsDtsServer130 | | | | Network login profile settings for MsDtsServer130 on NT SERVICE |
| | | | NT SERVICE\MSSQLSERVER | | | | Network login profile settings for MSSQLSERVER on NT SERVICE |
| | | | IIS APPPOOL\Classic .NET AppPool | | | | Network login profile settings for Classic .NET AppPool on IIS APPPOOL |
| | | | IIS APPPOOL\.NET v4.5 | | | | Network login profile settings for .NET v4.5 on IIS APPPOOL |
| | | | IIS APPPOOL\.NET v2.0 | | | | Network login profile settings for .NET v2.0 on IIS APPPOOL |
| | | | IIS APPPOOL\.NET v4.5 Classic | | | | Network login profile settings for .NET v4.5 Classic on IIS APPPOOL |
| | | | IIS APPPOOL\.NET v2.0 Classic | | | | Network login profile settings for .NET v2.0 Classic on IIS APPPOOL |

## Oscillating:

| Availability | BytesPerSector | Capabilities | CapabilityDescriptions | Caption | CompressionMethod | ConfigManagerErrorCode | ConfigManagerUserConfig |
|---|---|---|---|---|---|---|---|
| | 512 | 3, 4, 10 | Random Access, Supports Writing, SMART Notification | OCZ REVODRIVE350 SCSI Disk Device | | 0 | FALSE |
| | 512 | 3, 4 | Random Access, Supports Writing | NVMe TOSHIBA-RD400 | | 0 | FALSE |
| | 512 | 3, 4, 10 | Random Access, Supports Writing, SMART Notification | TOSHIBA DT01ACA200 | | 0 | FALSE |

## 3D:

| Availability | BytesPerSector | Capabilities | CapabilityDescriptions | Caption | CompressionMethod | ConfigManagerErrorCode | ConfigManagerUserConfig | CreationClassName |
|---|---|---|---|---|---|---|---|---|
| | 512 | 3, 4, 10 | Random Access, Supports Writing, SMART Notification | OCZ REVODRIVE350 SCSI Disk Device | | 0 | FALSE | Win32_DiskDrive |
| | 512 | 3, 4 | Random Access, Supports Writing | NVMe TOSHIBA-RD400 | | 0 | FALSE | Win32_DiskDrive |
| | 512 | 3, 4, 10 | Random Access, Supports Writing, SMART Notification | TOSHIBA DT01ACA200 | | 0 | FALSE | Win32_DiskDrive |

## Shadow Box:

| Availability | BytesPerSector | Capabilities | CapabilityDescriptions | Caption | CompressionMethod | ConfigManagerErrorCode | ConfigManagerUserConfig | CreationClassName | DefaultBlockSize |
|---|---|---|---|---|---|---|---|---|---|
| | 512 | 3, 4, 10 | Random Access, Supports Writing, SMART Notification | OCZ REVODRIVE350 SCSI Disk Device | | 0 | FALSE | Win32_DiskDrive | |
| | 512 | 3, 4 | Random Access, Supports Writing | NVMe TOSHIBA-RD400 | | 0 | FALSE | Win32_DiskDrive | |
| | 512 | 3, 4, 10 | Random Access, Supports Writing, SMART Notification | TOSHIBA DT01ACA200 | | 0 | FALSE | Win32_DiskDrive | |

Shadow Box Single Line Vertical

| BiosCharacteristics | 7, 10, 11, 12, 15, 16, 17, 19, 23, 24, 25, 26, 27, 28, 29, 32, 33, 40, 42, 43, 48, 50, 58, 59, 64, 65, 66, 67, 68, 69, 70, 71, 72, 73, 74, 75, 76, 77, 78, 79 |
| --- | --- |
| BIOSVersion | ALASKA - 1072009, 0504, American Megatrends - 5000C |
| BuildNumber | |
| Caption | 0504 |
| CodeSet | |
| CurrentLanguage | en\|US\|iso8859-1 |
| Description | 0504 |
| IdentificationCode | |
| InstallableLanguages | 8 |
| InstallDate | |
| LanguageEdition | |
| ListOfLanguages | en\|US\|iso8859-1, fr\|FR\|iso8859-1, zh\|CN\|unicode, , , , , |
| Manufacturer | American Megatrends Inc. |
| Name | 0504 |
| OtherTargetOS | |
| PrimaryBIOS | TRUE |

Shadow Box Multi line Vertical

| | | | |
|---|---|---|---|
| Availability | | | |
| BytesPerSector | 512 | 512 | 512 |
| Capabilities | 3, 4, 10 | 3, 4 | 3, 4, 10 |
| CapabilityDescriptions | Random Access, Supports Writing, SMART Notification | Random Access, Supports Writing | Random Access, Supports Writing, SMART Notification |
| Caption | OCZ REVODRIVE350 SCSI Disk Device | NVMe TOSHIBA RD400 | TOSHIBA DT01ACA200 |
| CompressionMethod | | | |
| ConfigManagerErrorCode | 0 | 0 | 0 |
| ConfigManagerUserConfig | FALSE | FALSE | FALSE |
| CreationClassName | Win32_DiskDrive | Win32_DiskDrive | Win32_DiskDrive |
| DefaultBlockSize | | | |
| Description | Disk drive | Disk drive | Disk drive |
| DeviceID | \\.\PHYSICALDRIVE2 | \\.\PHYSICALDRIVE1 | \\.\PHYSICALDRIVE0 |
| ErrorCleared | | | |
| ErrorDescription | | | |
| ErrorMethodology | | | |
| FirmwareRevision | 2.50 | 57CZ4102 | MX6OAB00 |
| Index | 2 | 1 | 0 |

118

# Stylesheets
## Decorating your web pages

BELOW ARE SOME STYLESHEETS I COOKED UP THAT I LIKE AND THINK YOU MIGHT TOO. Don't worry I won't be offended if you take and modify to your hearts delight. Please do!

NONE

```
$txtstream.WriteLine("<style type='text/css'>")
$txtstream.WriteLine("th")
$txtstream.WriteLine("{")
$txtstream.WriteLine("    COLOR: white;")
$txtstream.WriteLine("}")
$txtstream.WriteLine("td")
$txtstream.WriteLine("{")
$txtstream.WriteLine("    COLOR: white;")
$txtstream.WriteLine("}")
$txtstream.WriteLine("</style>")
```

```
$txtstream.WriteLine("<style type='text/css'>")
$txtstream.WriteLine("th")
$txtstream.WriteLine("{")
$txtstream.WriteLine("   COLOR: white;")
$txtstream.WriteLine("   BACKGROUND-COLOR: black;")
$txtstream.WriteLine("   FONT-FAMILY:font-family: Cambria, serif;")
$txtstream.WriteLine("   FONT-SIZE: 12px;")
$txtstream.WriteLine("   text-align: left;")
$txtstream.WriteLine("   white-Space: nowrap;")
$txtstream.WriteLine("}")
$txtstream.WriteLine("td")
$txtstream.WriteLine("{")
$txtstream.WriteLine("   COLOR: white;")
$txtstream.WriteLine("   BACKGROUND-COLOR: black;")
$txtstream.WriteLine("   FONT-FAMILY: font-family: Cambria, serif;")
$txtstream.WriteLine("   FONT-SIZE: 12px;")
$txtstream.WriteLine("   text-align: left;")
$txtstream.WriteLine("   white-Space: nowrap;")
$txtstream.WriteLine("}")
$txtstream.WriteLine("div")
$txtstream.WriteLine("{")
$txtstream.WriteLine("   COLOR: white;")
$txtstream.WriteLine("   BACKGROUND-COLOR: black;")
$txtstream.WriteLine("   FONT-FAMILY: font-family: Cambria, serif;")
$txtstream.WriteLine("   FONT-SIZE: 10px;")
$txtstream.WriteLine("   text-align: left;")
$txtstream.WriteLine("   white-Space: nowrap;")
$txtstream.WriteLine("}")
$txtstream.WriteLine("span")
$txtstream.WriteLine("{")
$txtstream.WriteLine("   COLOR: white;")
```

```
$txtstream.WriteLine("    BACKGROUND-COLOR: black;")
$txtstream.WriteLine("    FONT-FAMILY: font-family: Cambria, serif;")
$txtstream.WriteLine("    FONT-SIZE: 10px;")
$txtstream.WriteLine("    text-align: left;")
$txtstream.WriteLine("    white-Space: nowrap;")
$txtstream.WriteLine("    display:inline-block;")
$txtstream.WriteLine("    width: 100%;")
$txtstream.WriteLine("}")
$txtstream.WriteLine("textarea")
$txtstream.WriteLine("{")
$txtstream.WriteLine("    COLOR: white;")
$txtstream.WriteLine("    BACKGROUND-COLOR: black;")
$txtstream.WriteLine("    FONT-FAMILY: font-family: Cambria, serif;")
$txtstream.WriteLine("    FONT-SIZE: 10px;")
$txtstream.WriteLine("    text-align: left;")
$txtstream.WriteLine("    white-Space: nowrap;")
$txtstream.WriteLine("    width: 100%;")
$txtstream.WriteLine("}")
$txtstream.WriteLine("select")
$txtstream.WriteLine("{")
$txtstream.WriteLine("    COLOR: white;")
$txtstream.WriteLine("    BACKGROUND-COLOR: black;")
$txtstream.WriteLine("    FONT-FAMILY: font-family: Cambria, serif;")
$txtstream.WriteLine("    FONT-SIZE: 10px;")
$txtstream.WriteLine("    text-align: left;")
$txtstream.WriteLine("    white-Space: nowrap;")
$txtstream.WriteLine("    width: 100%;")
$txtstream.WriteLine("}")
$txtstream.WriteLine("input")
$txtstream.WriteLine("{")
$txtstream.WriteLine("    COLOR: white;")
$txtstream.WriteLine("    BACKGROUND-COLOR: black;")
$txtstream.WriteLine("    FONT-FAMILY: font-family: Cambria, serif;")
```

```
$txtstream.WriteLine("    FONT-SIZE: 12px;")
$txtstream.WriteLine("    text-align: left;")
$txtstream.WriteLine("    display:table-cell;")
$txtstream.WriteLine("    white-Space: nowrap;")
$txtstream.WriteLine("}")
$txtstream.WriteLine("h1 {")
$txtstream.WriteLine("color: antiquewhite;")
$txtstream.WriteLine("text-shadow: 1px 1px 1px black;")
$txtstream.WriteLine("padding: 3px;")
$txtstream.WriteLine("text-align: center;")
$txtstream.WriteLine("box-shadow: inset 2px 2px 5px rgba(0,0,0,0.5), inset -2px -2px 5px rgba(255,255,255,0.5)")
$txtstream.WriteLine("}")
$txtstream.WriteLine("</style>")
```

COLORED TEXT

```
$txtstream.WriteLine("<style type='text/css'>")
$txtstream.WriteLine("th")
$txtstream.WriteLine("{")
$txtstream.WriteLine("    COLOR: darkred;")
$txtstream.WriteLine("    BACKGROUND-COLOR: #eeeeee;")
$txtstream.WriteLine("    FONT-FAMILY:font-family: Cambria, serif;")
$txtstream.WriteLine("    FONT-SIZE: 12px;")
$txtstream.WriteLine("    text-align: left;")
$txtstream.WriteLine("    white-Space: nowrap;")
$txtstream.WriteLine("}")
$txtstream.WriteLine("td")
$txtstream.WriteLine("{")
$txtstream.WriteLine("    COLOR: navy;")
$txtstream.WriteLine("    BACKGROUND-COLOR: #eeeeee;")
$txtstream.WriteLine("    FONT-FAMILY: font-family: Cambria, serif;")
$txtstream.WriteLine("    FONT-SIZE: 12px;")
```

```
$txtstream.WriteLine("    text-align: left;")
$txtstream.WriteLine("    white-Space: nowrap;")
$txtstream.WriteLine("}")
$txtstream.WriteLine("div")
$txtstream.WriteLine("{")
$txtstream.WriteLine("    COLOR: white;")
$txtstream.WriteLine("    BACKGROUND-COLOR: navy;")
$txtstream.WriteLine("    FONT-FAMILY: font-family: Cambria, serif;")
$txtstream.WriteLine("    FONT-SIZE: 10px;")
$txtstream.WriteLine("    text-align: left;")
$txtstream.WriteLine("    white-Space: nowrap;")
$txtstream.WriteLine("}")
$txtstream.WriteLine("span")
$txtstream.WriteLine("{")
$txtstream.WriteLine("    COLOR: white;")
$txtstream.WriteLine("    BACKGROUND-COLOR: navy;")
$txtstream.WriteLine("    FONT-FAMILY: font-family: Cambria, serif;")
$txtstream.WriteLine("    FONT-SIZE: 10px;")
$txtstream.WriteLine("    text-align: left;")
$txtstream.WriteLine("    white-Space: nowrap;")
$txtstream.WriteLine("    display:inline-block;")
$txtstream.WriteLine("    width: 100%;")
$txtstream.WriteLine("}")
$txtstream.WriteLine("textarea")
$txtstream.WriteLine("{")
$txtstream.WriteLine("    COLOR: white;")
$txtstream.WriteLine("    BACKGROUND-COLOR: navy;")
$txtstream.WriteLine("    FONT-FAMILY: font-family: Cambria, serif;")
$txtstream.WriteLine("    FONT-SIZE: 10px;")
$txtstream.WriteLine("    text-align: left;")
$txtstream.WriteLine("    white-Space: nowrap;")
$txtstream.WriteLine("    width: 100%;")
$txtstream.WriteLine("}")
```

```
$txtstream.WriteLine("select")
$txtstream.WriteLine("{")
$txtstream.WriteLine("   COLOR: white;")
$txtstream.WriteLine("   BACKGROUND-COLOR: navy;")
$txtstream.WriteLine("   FONT-FAMILY: font-family: Cambria, serif;")
$txtstream.WriteLine("   FONT-SIZE: 10px;")
$txtstream.WriteLine("   text-align: left;")
$txtstream.WriteLine("   white-Space: nowrap;")
$txtstream.WriteLine("   width: 100%;")
$txtstream.WriteLine("}")
$txtstream.WriteLine("input")
$txtstream.WriteLine("{")
$txtstream.WriteLine("   COLOR: white;")
$txtstream.WriteLine("   BACKGROUND-COLOR: navy;")
$txtstream.WriteLine("   FONT-FAMILY: font-family: Cambria, serif;")
$txtstream.WriteLine("   FONT-SIZE: 12px;")
$txtstream.WriteLine("   text-align: left;")
$txtstream.WriteLine("   display:table-cell;")
$txtstream.WriteLine("   white-Space: nowrap;")
$txtstream.WriteLine("}")
$txtstream.WriteLine("h1 {")
$txtstream.WriteLine("color: antiquewhite;")
$txtstream.WriteLine("text-shadow: 1px 1px 1px black;")
$txtstream.WriteLine("padding: 3px;")
$txtstream.WriteLine("text-align: center;")
$txtstream.WriteLine("box-shadow: inset 2px 2px 5px rgba(0,0,0,0.5), inset -
2px -2px 5px rgba(255,255,255,0.5)")
$txtstream.WriteLine("}")
$txtstream.WriteLine("</style>")
```

OSCILLATING ROW COLORS

```
$txtstream.WriteLine("<style>")
$txtstream.WriteLine("th")
$txtstream.WriteLine("{")
$txtstream.WriteLine("   COLOR: white;")
$txtstream.WriteLine("   BACKGROUND-COLOR: navy;")
$txtstream.WriteLine("   FONT-FAMILY:font-family: Cambria, serif;")
$txtstream.WriteLine("   FONT-SIZE: 12px;")
$txtstream.WriteLine("   text-align: left;")
$txtstream.WriteLine("   white-Space: nowrap;")
$txtstream.WriteLine("}")
$txtstream.WriteLine("td")
$txtstream.WriteLine("{")
$txtstream.WriteLine("   COLOR: navy;")
$txtstream.WriteLine("   FONT-FAMILY: font-family: Cambria, serif;")
$txtstream.WriteLine("   FONT-SIZE: 12px;")
$txtstream.WriteLine("   text-align: left;")
$txtstream.WriteLine("   white-Space: nowrap;")
$txtstream.WriteLine("}")
$txtstream.WriteLine("div")
$txtstream.WriteLine("{")
$txtstream.WriteLine("   COLOR: navy;")
$txtstream.WriteLine("   FONT-FAMILY: font-family: Cambria, serif;")
$txtstream.WriteLine("   FONT-SIZE: 12px;")
$txtstream.WriteLine("   text-align: left;")
$txtstream.WriteLine("   white-Space: nowrap;")
$txtstream.WriteLine("}")
$txtstream.WriteLine("span")
$txtstream.WriteLine("{")
$txtstream.WriteLine("   COLOR: navy;")
$txtstream.WriteLine("   FONT-FAMILY: font-family: Cambria, serif;")
$txtstream.WriteLine("   FONT-SIZE: 12px;")
$txtstream.WriteLine("   text-align: left;")
```

```
$txtstream.WriteLine("    white-Space: nowrap;")
$txtstream.WriteLine("    width: 100%;")
$txtstream.WriteLine("}")
$txtstream.WriteLine("textarea")
$txtstream.WriteLine("{")
$txtstream.WriteLine("    COLOR: navy;")
$txtstream.WriteLine("    FONT-FAMILY: font-family: Cambria, serif;")
$txtstream.WriteLine("    FONT-SIZE: 12px;")
$txtstream.WriteLine("    text-align: left;")
$txtstream.WriteLine("    white-Space: nowrap;")
$txtstream.WriteLine("    display:inline-block;")
$txtstream.WriteLine("    width: 100%;")
$txtstream.WriteLine("}")
$txtstream.WriteLine("select")
$txtstream.WriteLine("{")
$txtstream.WriteLine("    COLOR: navy;")
$txtstream.WriteLine("    FONT-FAMILY: font-family: Cambria, serif;")
$txtstream.WriteLine("    FONT-SIZE: 10px;")
$txtstream.WriteLine("    text-align: left;")
$txtstream.WriteLine("    white-Space: nowrap;")
$txtstream.WriteLine("    display:inline-block;")
$txtstream.WriteLine("    width: 100%;")
$txtstream.WriteLine("}")
$txtstream.WriteLine("input")
$txtstream.WriteLine("{")
$txtstream.WriteLine("    COLOR: navy;")
$txtstream.WriteLine("    FONT-FAMILY: font-family: Cambria, serif;")
$txtstream.WriteLine("    FONT-SIZE: 12px;")
$txtstream.WriteLine("    text-align: left;")
$txtstream.WriteLine("    display:table-cell;")
$txtstream.WriteLine("    white-Space: nowrap;")
$txtstream.WriteLine("}")
$txtstream.WriteLine("h1 {")
```

```
$txtstream.WriteLine("color: antiquewhite;")
$txtstream.WriteLine("text-shadow: 1px 1px 1px black;")
$txtstream.WriteLine("padding: 3px;")
$txtstream.WriteLine("text-align: center;")
$txtstream.WriteLine("box-shadow: inset 2px 2px 5px rgba(0,0,0,0.5), inset -
2px -2px 5px rgba(255,255,255,0.5)")
$txtstream.WriteLine("}")
$txtstream.WriteLine("tr:nth-child(even){background-color:#f2f2f2;}")
$txtstream.WriteLine("tr:nth-child(odd){background-color:#cccccc;
color:#f2f2f2;}")
$txtstream.WriteLine("</style>")
```

GHOST DECORATED

```
$txtstream.WriteLine("<style type='text/css'>")
$txtstream.WriteLine("th")
$txtstream.WriteLine("{")
$txtstream.WriteLine("    COLOR: black;")
$txtstream.WriteLine("    BACKGROUND-COLOR: white;")
$txtstream.WriteLine("    FONT-FAMILY:font-family: Cambria, serif;")
$txtstream.WriteLine("    FONT-SIZE: 12px;")
$txtstream.WriteLine("    text-align: left;")
$txtstream.WriteLine("    white-Space: nowrap;")
$txtstream.WriteLine("}")
$txtstream.WriteLine("td")
$txtstream.WriteLine("{")
$txtstream.WriteLine("    COLOR: black;")
$txtstream.WriteLine("    BACKGROUND-COLOR: white;")
$txtstream.WriteLine("    FONT-FAMILY: font-family: Cambria, serif;")
$txtstream.WriteLine("    FONT-SIZE: 12px;")
$txtstream.WriteLine("    text-align: left;")
$txtstream.WriteLine("    white-Space: nowrap;")
$txtstream.WriteLine("}")
```

```
$txtstream.WriteLine("div")
$txtstream.WriteLine("{")
$txtstream.WriteLine("   COLOR: black;")
$txtstream.WriteLine("   BACKGROUND-COLOR: white;")
$txtstream.WriteLine("   FONT-FAMILY: font-family: Cambria, serif;")
$txtstream.WriteLine("   FONT-SIZE: 10px;")
$txtstream.WriteLine("   text-align: left;")
$txtstream.WriteLine("   white-Space: nowrap;")
$txtstream.WriteLine("}")
$txtstream.WriteLine("span")
$txtstream.WriteLine("{")
$txtstream.WriteLine("   COLOR: black;")
$txtstream.WriteLine("   BACKGROUND-COLOR: white;")
$txtstream.WriteLine("   FONT-FAMILY: font-family: Cambria, serif;")
$txtstream.WriteLine("   FONT-SIZE: 10px;")
$txtstream.WriteLine("   text-align: left;")
$txtstream.WriteLine("   white-Space: nowrap;")
$txtstream.WriteLine("   display:inline-block;")
$txtstream.WriteLine("   width: 100%;")
$txtstream.WriteLine("}")
$txtstream.WriteLine("textarea")
$txtstream.WriteLine("{")
$txtstream.WriteLine("   COLOR: black;")
$txtstream.WriteLine("   BACKGROUND-COLOR: white;")
$txtstream.WriteLine("   FONT-FAMILY: font-family: Cambria, serif;")
$txtstream.WriteLine("   FONT-SIZE: 10px;")
$txtstream.WriteLine("   text-align: left;")
$txtstream.WriteLine("   white-Space: nowrap;")
$txtstream.WriteLine("   width: 100%;")
$txtstream.WriteLine("}")
$txtstream.WriteLine("select")
$txtstream.WriteLine("{")
$txtstream.WriteLine("   COLOR: black;")
```

```
$txtstream.WriteLine("    BACKGROUND-COLOR: white;")
$txtstream.WriteLine("    FONT-FAMILY: font-family: Cambria, serif;")
$txtstream.WriteLine("    FONT-SIZE: 10px;")
$txtstream.WriteLine("    text-align: left;")
$txtstream.WriteLine("    white-Space: nowrap;")
$txtstream.WriteLine("    width: 100%;")
$txtstream.WriteLine("}")
$txtstream.WriteLine("input")
$txtstream.WriteLine("{")
$txtstream.WriteLine("    COLOR: black;")
$txtstream.WriteLine("    BACKGROUND-COLOR: white;")
$txtstream.WriteLine("    FONT-FAMILY: font-family: Cambria, serif;")
$txtstream.WriteLine("    FONT-SIZE: 12px;")
$txtstream.WriteLine("    text-align: left;")
$txtstream.WriteLine("    display:table-cell;")
$txtstream.WriteLine("    white-Space: nowrap;")
$txtstream.WriteLine("}")
$txtstream.WriteLine("h1 {")
$txtstream.WriteLine("color: antiquewhite;")
$txtstream.WriteLine("text-shadow: 1px 1px 1px black;")
$txtstream.WriteLine("padding: 3px;")
$txtstream.WriteLine("text-align: center;")
$txtstream.WriteLine("box-shadow: inset 2px 2px 5px rgba(0,0,0,0.5), inset -
2px -2px 5px rgba(255,255,255,0.5)")
$txtstream.WriteLine("}")
$txtstream.WriteLine("</style>")
```

3D

```
$txtstream.WriteLine("<style type='text/css'>")
$txtstream.WriteLine("body")
$txtstream.WriteLine("{")
```

129

```
$txtstream.WriteLine("    PADDING-RIGHT: 0px;")
$txtstream.WriteLine("    PADDING-LEFT: 0px;")
$txtstream.WriteLine("    PADDING-BOTTOM: 0px;")
$txtstream.WriteLine("    MARGIN: 0px;")
$txtstream.WriteLine("    COLOR: #333;")
$txtstream.WriteLine("    PADDING-TOP: 0px;")
$txtstream.WriteLine("    FONT-FAMILY: verdana, arial, helvetica, sans-
serif;")
$txtstream.WriteLine("}")
$txtstream.WriteLine("table")
$txtstream.WriteLine("{")
$txtstream.WriteLine("    BORDER-RIGHT: #999999 3px solid;")
$txtstream.WriteLine("    PADDING-RIGHT: 6px;")
$txtstream.WriteLine("    PADDING-LEFT: 6px;")
$txtstream.WriteLine("    FONT-WEIGHT: Bold;")
$txtstream.WriteLine("    FONT-SIZE: 14px;")
$txtstream.WriteLine("    PADDING-BOTTOM: 6px;")
$txtstream.WriteLine("    COLOR: Peru;")
$txtstream.WriteLine("    LINE-HEIGHT: 14px;")
$txtstream.WriteLine("    PADDING-TOP: 6px;")
$txtstream.WriteLine("    BORDER-BOTTOM: #999 1px solid;")
$txtstream.WriteLine("    BACKGROUND-COLOR: #eeeeee;")
$txtstream.WriteLine("    FONT-FAMILY: verdana, arial, helvetica, sans-
serif;")
$txtstream.WriteLine("    FONT-SIZE: 12px;")
$txtstream.WriteLine("}")
$txtstream.WriteLine("th")
$txtstream.WriteLine("{")
$txtstream.WriteLine("    BORDER-RIGHT: #999999 3px solid;")
$txtstream.WriteLine("    PADDING-RIGHT: 6px;")
$txtstream.WriteLine("    PADDING-LEFT: 6px;")
$txtstream.WriteLine("    FONT-WEIGHT: Bold;")
$txtstream.WriteLine("    FONT-SIZE: 14px;")
```

```
$txtstream.WriteLine("    PADDING-BOTTOM: 6px;")
$txtstream.WriteLine("    COLOR: darkred;")
$txtstream.WriteLine("    LINE-HEIGHT: 14px;")
$txtstream.WriteLine("    PADDING-TOP: 6px;")
$txtstream.WriteLine("    BORDER-BOTTOM: #999 1px solid;")
$txtstream.WriteLine("    BACKGROUND-COLOR: #eeeeee;")
$txtstream.WriteLine("    FONT-FAMILY:font-family: Cambria, serif;")
$txtstream.WriteLine("    FONT-SIZE: 12px;")
$txtstream.WriteLine("    text-align: left;")
$txtstream.WriteLine("    white-Space: nowrap;")
$txtstream.WriteLine("}")
$txtstream.WriteLine(".th")
$txtstream.WriteLine("{")
$txtstream.WriteLine("    BORDER-RIGHT: #999999 2px solid;")
$txtstream.WriteLine("    PADDING-RIGHT: 6px;")
$txtstream.WriteLine("    PADDING-LEFT: 6px;")
$txtstream.WriteLine("    FONT-WEIGHT: Bold;")
$txtstream.WriteLine("    PADDING-BOTTOM: 6px;")
$txtstream.WriteLine("    COLOR: black;")
$txtstream.WriteLine("    PADDING-TOP: 6px;")
$txtstream.WriteLine("    BORDER-BOTTOM: #999 2px solid;")
$txtstream.WriteLine("    BACKGROUND-COLOR: #eeeeee;")
$txtstream.WriteLine("    FONT-FAMILY: font-family: Cambria, serif;")
$txtstream.WriteLine("    FONT-SIZE: 10px;")
$txtstream.WriteLine("    text-align: right;")
$txtstream.WriteLine("    white-Space: nowrap;")
$txtstream.WriteLine("}")
$txtstream.WriteLine("td")
$txtstream.WriteLine("{")
$txtstream.WriteLine("    BORDER-RIGHT: #999999 3px solid;")
$txtstream.WriteLine("    PADDING-RIGHT: 6px;")
$txtstream.WriteLine("    PADDING-LEFT: 6px;")
$txtstream.WriteLine("    FONT-WEIGHT: Normal;")
```

```
$txtstream.WriteLine("    PADDING-BOTTOM: 6px;")
$txtstream.WriteLine("    COLOR: navy;")
$txtstream.WriteLine("    LINE-HEIGHT: 14px;")
$txtstream.WriteLine("    PADDING-TOP: 6px;")
$txtstream.WriteLine("    BORDER-BOTTOM: #999 1px solid;")
$txtstream.WriteLine("    BACKGROUND-COLOR: #eeeeee;")
$txtstream.WriteLine("    FONT-FAMILY: font-family: Cambria, serif;")
$txtstream.WriteLine("    FONT-SIZE: 12px;")
$txtstream.WriteLine("    text-align: left;")
$txtstream.WriteLine("    white-Space: nowrap;")
$txtstream.WriteLine("}")
$txtstream.WriteLine("div")
$txtstream.WriteLine("{")
$txtstream.WriteLine("    BORDER-RIGHT: #999999 3px solid;")
$txtstream.WriteLine("    PADDING-RIGHT: 6px;")
$txtstream.WriteLine("    PADDING-LEFT: 6px;")
$txtstream.WriteLine("    FONT-WEIGHT: Normal;")
$txtstream.WriteLine("    PADDING-BOTTOM: 6px;")
$txtstream.WriteLine("    COLOR: white;")
$txtstream.WriteLine("    PADDING-TOP: 6px;")
$txtstream.WriteLine("    BORDER-BOTTOM: #999 1px solid;")
$txtstream.WriteLine("    BACKGROUND-COLOR: navy;")
$txtstream.WriteLine("    FONT-FAMILY: font-family: Cambria, serif;")
$txtstream.WriteLine("    FONT-SIZE: 10px;")
$txtstream.WriteLine("    text-align: left;")
$txtstream.WriteLine("    white-Space: nowrap;")
$txtstream.WriteLine("}")
$txtstream.WriteLine("span")
$txtstream.WriteLine("{")
$txtstream.WriteLine("    BORDER-RIGHT: #999999 3px solid;")
$txtstream.WriteLine("    PADDING-RIGHT: 3px;")
$txtstream.WriteLine("    PADDING-LEFT: 3px;")
$txtstream.WriteLine("    FONT-WEIGHT: Normal;")
```

```
$txtstream.WriteLine("   PADDING-BOTTOM: 3px;")
$txtstream.WriteLine("   COLOR: white;")
$txtstream.WriteLine("   PADDING-TOP: 3px;")
$txtstream.WriteLine("   BORDER-BOTTOM: #999 1px solid;")
$txtstream.WriteLine("   BACKGROUND-COLOR: navy;")
$txtstream.WriteLine("   FONT-FAMILY: font-family: Cambria, serif;")
$txtstream.WriteLine("   FONT-SIZE: 10px;")
$txtstream.WriteLine("   text-align: left;")
$txtstream.WriteLine("   white-Space: nowrap;")
$txtstream.WriteLine("   display:inline-block;")
$txtstream.WriteLine("   width: 100%;")
$txtstream.WriteLine("}")
$txtstream.WriteLine("textarea")
$txtstream.WriteLine("{")
$txtstream.WriteLine("   BORDER-RIGHT: #999999 3px solid;")
$txtstream.WriteLine("   PADDING-RIGHT: 3px;")
$txtstream.WriteLine("   PADDING-LEFT: 3px;")
$txtstream.WriteLine("   FONT-WEIGHT: Normal;")
$txtstream.WriteLine("   PADDING-BOTTOM: 3px;")
$txtstream.WriteLine("   COLOR: white;")
$txtstream.WriteLine("   PADDING-TOP: 3px;")
$txtstream.WriteLine("   BORDER-BOTTOM: #999 1px solid;")
$txtstream.WriteLine("   BACKGROUND-COLOR: navy;")
$txtstream.WriteLine("   FONT-FAMILY: font-family: Cambria, serif;")
$txtstream.WriteLine("   FONT-SIZE: 10px;")
$txtstream.WriteLine("   text-align: left;")
$txtstream.WriteLine("   white-Space: nowrap;")
$txtstream.WriteLine("   width: 100%;")
$txtstream.WriteLine("}")
$txtstream.WriteLine("select")
$txtstream.WriteLine("{")
$txtstream.WriteLine("   BORDER-RIGHT: #999999 3px solid;")
$txtstream.WriteLine("   PADDING-RIGHT: 6px;")
```

```
$txtstream.WriteLine("    PADDING-LEFT: 6px;")
$txtstream.WriteLine("    FONT-WEIGHT: Normal;")
$txtstream.WriteLine("    PADDING-BOTTOM: 6px;")
$txtstream.WriteLine("    COLOR: white;")
$txtstream.WriteLine("    PADDING-TOP: 6px;")
$txtstream.WriteLine("    BORDER-BOTTOM: #999 1px solid;")
$txtstream.WriteLine("    BACKGROUND-COLOR: navy;")
$txtstream.WriteLine("    FONT-FAMILY: font-family: Cambria, serif;")
$txtstream.WriteLine("    FONT-SIZE: 10px;")
$txtstream.WriteLine("    text-align: left;")
$txtstream.WriteLine("    white-Space: nowrap;")
$txtstream.WriteLine("    width: 100%;")
$txtstream.WriteLine("}")
$txtstream.WriteLine("input")
$txtstream.WriteLine("{")
$txtstream.WriteLine("    BORDER-RIGHT: #999999 3px solid;")
$txtstream.WriteLine("    PADDING-RIGHT: 3px;")
$txtstream.WriteLine("    PADDING-LEFT: 3px;")
$txtstream.WriteLine("    FONT-WEIGHT: Bold;")
$txtstream.WriteLine("    PADDING-BOTTOM: 3px;")
$txtstream.WriteLine("    COLOR: white;")
$txtstream.WriteLine("    PADDING-TOP: 3px;")
$txtstream.WriteLine("    BORDER-BOTTOM: #999 1px solid;")
$txtstream.WriteLine("    BACKGROUND-COLOR: navy;")
$txtstream.WriteLine("    FONT-FAMILY: font-family: Cambria, serif;")
$txtstream.WriteLine("    FONT-SIZE: 12px;")
$txtstream.WriteLine("    text-align: left;")
$txtstream.WriteLine("    display:table-cell;")
$txtstream.WriteLine("    white-Space: nowrap;")
$txtstream.WriteLine("    width: 100%;")
$txtstream.WriteLine("}")
$txtstream.WriteLine("h1 {")
$txtstream.WriteLine("color: antiquewhite;")
```

```
$txtstream.WriteLine("text-shadow: 1px 1px 1px black;")
$txtstream.WriteLine("padding: 3px;")
$txtstream.WriteLine("text-align: center;")
$txtstream.WriteLine("box-shadow: inset 2px 2px 5px rgba(0,0,0,0.5), inset -
2px -2px 5px rgba(255,255,255,0.5)")
$txtstream.WriteLine("}")
$txtstream.WriteLine("</style>")
```

## SHADOW BOX

```
$txtstream.WriteLine("<style type='text/css'>")
$txtstream.WriteLine("body")
$txtstream.WriteLine("{")
$txtstream.WriteLine("   PADDING-RIGHT: 0px;")
$txtstream.WriteLine("   PADDING-LEFT: 0px;")
$txtstream.WriteLine("   PADDING-BOTTOM: 0px;")
$txtstream.WriteLine("   MARGIN: 0px;")
$txtstream.WriteLine("   COLOR: #333;")
$txtstream.WriteLine("   PADDING-TOP: 0px;")
$txtstream.WriteLine("   FONT-FAMILY: verdana, arial, helvetica, sans-
serif;")
$txtstream.WriteLine("}")
$txtstream.WriteLine("table")
$txtstream.WriteLine("{")
$txtstream.WriteLine("   BORDER-RIGHT: #999999 1px solid;")
$txtstream.WriteLine("   PADDING-RIGHT: 1px;")
$txtstream.WriteLine("   PADDING-LEFT: 1px;")
$txtstream.WriteLine("   PADDING-BOTTOM: 1px;")
$txtstream.WriteLine("   LINE-HEIGHT: 8px;")
$txtstream.WriteLine("   PADDING-TOP: 1px;")
$txtstream.WriteLine("   BORDER-BOTTOM: #999 1px solid;")
$txtstream.WriteLine("   BACKGROUND-COLOR: #eeeeee;")
```

$txtstream.WriteLine("

filter:progid:DXImageTransform.Microsoft.Shadow(color='silver', Direction=135, Strength=16)")

$txtstream.WriteLine("}")

$txtstream.WriteLine("th")

$txtstream.WriteLine("{")

$txtstream.WriteLine("    BORDER-RIGHT: #999999 3px solid;")

$txtstream.WriteLine("    PADDING-RIGHT: 6px;")

$txtstream.WriteLine("    PADDING-LEFT: 6px;")

$txtstream.WriteLine("    FONT-WEIGHT: Bold;")

$txtstream.WriteLine("    FONT-SIZE: 14px;")

$txtstream.WriteLine("    PADDING-BOTTOM: 6px;")

$txtstream.WriteLine("    COLOR: darkred;")

$txtstream.WriteLine("    LINE-HEIGHT: 14px;")

$txtstream.WriteLine("    PADDING-TOP: 6px;")

$txtstream.WriteLine("    BORDER-BOTTOM: #999 1px solid;")

$txtstream.WriteLine("    BACKGROUND-COLOR: #eeeeee;")

$txtstream.WriteLine("    FONT-FAMILY: font-family: Cambria, serif;")

$txtstream.WriteLine("    FONT-SIZE: 12px;")

$txtstream.WriteLine("    text-align: left;")

$txtstream.WriteLine("    white-Space: nowrap;")

$txtstream.WriteLine("}")

$txtstream.WriteLine(".th")

$txtstream.WriteLine("{")

$txtstream.WriteLine("    BORDER-RIGHT: #999999 2px solid;")

$txtstream.WriteLine("    PADDING-RIGHT: 6px;")

$txtstream.WriteLine("    PADDING-LEFT: 6px;")

$txtstream.WriteLine("    FONT-WEIGHT: Bold;")

$txtstream.WriteLine("    PADDING-BOTTOM: 6px;")

$txtstream.WriteLine("    COLOR: black;")

$txtstream.WriteLine("    PADDING-TOP: 6px;")

$txtstream.WriteLine("    BORDER-BOTTOM: #999 2px solid;")

$txtstream.WriteLine("    BACKGROUND-COLOR: #eeeeee;")

```
$txtstream.WriteLine("   FONT-FAMILY: font-family: Cambria, serif;")
$txtstream.WriteLine("   FONT-SIZE: 10px;")
$txtstream.WriteLine("   text-align: right;")
$txtstream.WriteLine("   white-Space: nowrap;")
$txtstream.WriteLine("}")
$txtstream.WriteLine("td")
$txtstream.WriteLine("{")
$txtstream.WriteLine("   BORDER-RIGHT: #999999 3px solid;")
$txtstream.WriteLine("   PADDING-RIGHT: 6px;")
$txtstream.WriteLine("   PADDING-LEFT: 6px;")
$txtstream.WriteLine("   FONT-WEIGHT: Normal;")
$txtstream.WriteLine("   PADDING-BOTTOM: 6px;")
$txtstream.WriteLine("   COLOR: navy;")
$txtstream.WriteLine("   LINE-HEIGHT: 14px;")
$txtstream.WriteLine("   PADDING-TOP: 6px;")
$txtstream.WriteLine("   BORDER-BOTTOM: #999 1px solid;")
$txtstream.WriteLine("   BACKGROUND-COLOR: #eeeeee;")
$txtstream.WriteLine("   FONT-FAMILY: font-family: Cambria, serif;")
$txtstream.WriteLine("   FONT-SIZE: 12px;")
$txtstream.WriteLine("   text-align: left;")
$txtstream.WriteLine("   white-Space: nowrap;")
$txtstream.WriteLine("}")
$txtstream.WriteLine("div")
$txtstream.WriteLine("{")
$txtstream.WriteLine("   BORDER-RIGHT: #999999 3px solid;")
$txtstream.WriteLine("   PADDING-RIGHT: 6px;")
$txtstream.WriteLine("   PADDING-LEFT: 6px;")
$txtstream.WriteLine("   FONT-WEIGHT: Normal;")
$txtstream.WriteLine("   PADDING-BOTTOM: 6px;")
$txtstream.WriteLine("   COLOR: white;")
$txtstream.WriteLine("   PADDING-TOP: 6px;")
$txtstream.WriteLine("   BORDER-BOTTOM: #999 1px solid;")
$txtstream.WriteLine("   BACKGROUND-COLOR: navy;")
```

$txtstream.WriteLine("    FONT-FAMILY: font-family: Cambria, serif;")
$txtstream.WriteLine("    FONT-SIZE: 10px;")
$txtstream.WriteLine("    text-align: left;")
$txtstream.WriteLine("    white-Space: nowrap;")
$txtstream.WriteLine("}")
$txtstream.WriteLine("span")
$txtstream.WriteLine("{")
$txtstream.WriteLine("    BORDER-RIGHT: #999999 3px solid;")
$txtstream.WriteLine("    PADDING-RIGHT: 3px;")
$txtstream.WriteLine("    PADDING-LEFT: 3px;")
$txtstream.WriteLine("    FONT-WEIGHT: Normal;")
$txtstream.WriteLine("    PADDING-BOTTOM: 3px;")
$txtstream.WriteLine("    COLOR: white;")
$txtstream.WriteLine("    PADDING-TOP: 3px;")
$txtstream.WriteLine("    BORDER-BOTTOM: #999 1px solid;")
$txtstream.WriteLine("    BACKGROUND-COLOR: navy;")
$txtstream.WriteLine("    FONT-FAMILY: font-family: Cambria, serif;")
$txtstream.WriteLine("    FONT-SIZE: 10px;")
$txtstream.WriteLine("    text-align: left;")
$txtstream.WriteLine("    white-Space: nowrap;")
$txtstream.WriteLine("    display: inline-block;")
$txtstream.WriteLine("    width: 100%;")
$txtstream.WriteLine("}")
$txtstream.WriteLine("textarea")
$txtstream.WriteLine("{")
$txtstream.WriteLine("    BORDER-RIGHT: #999999 3px solid;")
$txtstream.WriteLine("    PADDING-RIGHT: 3px;")
$txtstream.WriteLine("    PADDING-LEFT: 3px;")
$txtstream.WriteLine("    FONT-WEIGHT: Normal;")
$txtstream.WriteLine("    PADDING-BOTTOM: 3px;")
$txtstream.WriteLine("    COLOR: white;")
$txtstream.WriteLine("    PADDING-TOP: 3px;")
$txtstream.WriteLine("    BORDER-BOTTOM: #999 1px solid;")

```
$txtstream.WriteLine("    BACKGROUND-COLOR: navy;")
$txtstream.WriteLine("    FONT-FAMILY: font-family: Cambria, serif;")
$txtstream.WriteLine("    FONT-SIZE: 10px;")
$txtstream.WriteLine("    text-align: left;")
$txtstream.WriteLine("    white-Space: nowrap;")
$txtstream.WriteLine("    width: 100%;")
$txtstream.WriteLine("}")
$txtstream.WriteLine("select")
$txtstream.WriteLine("{")
$txtstream.WriteLine("    BORDER-RIGHT: #999999 3px solid;")
$txtstream.WriteLine("    PADDING-RIGHT: 6px;")
$txtstream.WriteLine("    PADDING-LEFT: 6px;")
$txtstream.WriteLine("    FONT-WEIGHT: Normal;")
$txtstream.WriteLine("    PADDING-BOTTOM: 6px;")
$txtstream.WriteLine("    COLOR: white;")
$txtstream.WriteLine("    PADDING-TOP: 6px;")
$txtstream.WriteLine("    BORDER-BOTTOM: #999 1px solid;")
$txtstream.WriteLine("    BACKGROUND-COLOR: navy;")
$txtstream.WriteLine("    FONT-FAMILY: font-family: Cambria, serif;")
$txtstream.WriteLine("    FONT-SIZE: 10px;")
$txtstream.WriteLine("    text-align: left;")
$txtstream.WriteLine("    white-Space: nowrap;")
$txtstream.WriteLine("    width: 100%;")
$txtstream.WriteLine("}")
$txtstream.WriteLine("input")
$txtstream.WriteLine("{")
$txtstream.WriteLine("    BORDER-RIGHT: #999999 3px solid;")
$txtstream.WriteLine("    PADDING-RIGHT: 3px;")
$txtstream.WriteLine("    PADDING-LEFT: 3px;")
$txtstream.WriteLine("    FONT-WEIGHT: Bold;")
$txtstream.WriteLine("    PADDING-BOTTOM: 3px;")
$txtstream.WriteLine("    COLOR: white;")
$txtstream.WriteLine("    PADDING-TOP: 3px;")
```

```
$txtstream.WriteLine("    BORDER-BOTTOM: #999 1px solid;")
$txtstream.WriteLine("    BACKGROUND-COLOR: navy;")
$txtstream.WriteLine("    FONT-FAMILY: font-family: Cambria, serif;")
$txtstream.WriteLine("    FONT-SIZE: 12px;")
$txtstream.WriteLine("    text-align: left;")
$txtstream.WriteLine("    display: table-cell;")
$txtstream.WriteLine("    white-Space: nowrap;")
$txtstream.WriteLine("    width: 100%;")
$txtstream.WriteLine("}")
$txtstream.WriteLine("h1 {")
$txtstream.WriteLine("color: antiquewhite;")
$txtstream.WriteLine("text-shadow: 1px 1px 1px black;")
$txtstream.WriteLine("padding: 3px;")
$txtstream.WriteLine("text-align: center;")
$txtstream.WriteLine("box-shadow: inset 2px 2px 5px rgba(0,0,0,0.5), inset -
2px -2px 5px rgba(255,255,255,0.5)")
$txtstream.WriteLine("}")
$txtstream.WriteLine("</style>")
```